Massachusetts 101

Massachusetts 101

The 101 Events That Made Massachusetts

CHRISTOPHER KENNEALLY

COMMONWEALTH EDITIONS
Beverly, Massachusetts

FOR CLAUDIA

WHO WILL MAKE HER OWN HISTORY

ISBN-13: 978-1-889833-36-1
ISBN-10: 1-889833-36-3

An earlier version of this book was published as *Massachusetts Legacy* in
1995 by Adams Media Corporation under ISBN 1-55850-528-8.

Library of Congress Cataloging-in-Publication Data
Kenneally, Christopher.
  Massachusetts 101 : 101 events that made Massachusetts / Christopher
Kenneally.
    p. cm.
  Shortened and edited ed. of: Massachusetts legacy. c1995.
  Includes bibliographical references and index.
  ISBN 1-889833-36-3
  1. Massachusetts—History—Anecdotes. I. Title: Massachusetts one
hundred one. II. Title: Massachusetts one hundred and one. III.
Kenneally, Christopher. Massachusetts legacy. IV. Title.
  F64.6.K46 2005
  974.4—dc22   2005005520

Cover and interior design by Ann Conneman.
Photographs by Ralph Turcotte.

Printed in Canada.

Commonwealth Editions
266 Cabot Street, Beverly, Massachusetts 01915
www.commonwealtheditions.com

Contents

ACKNOWLEDGMENTS x

PREFACE xi

1 MASSACHUSETTS reemerges as the Pleistocene ice sheet retreats 1

2 PALEO-INDIAN HUNTERS settle in Massachusetts 2

3 BARTHOLOMEW GOSNOLD explores the Massachusetts coast
and names Cape Cod 4

4 CAPT. JOHN SMITH maps the coastline between Cape Cod
Bay and Penobscot 5

5 THE MAYFLOWER, carrying the Pilgrims, arrives in Cape Cod Bay 6

6 THE PILGRIMS celebrate the first Thanksgiving 8

7 WILLIAM BLACKSTONE settles at Shawmut Peninsula, the
future site of Boston 10

8 JOHN WINTHROP leads Puritan ships into Massachusetts Bay 12

9 ANNE HUTCHINSON outrages Boston clergy 14

10 THE FIRST PUBLIC SCHOOL in America, the Boston Latin
School, is founded 16

11 THE GENERAL COURT establishes a "schoale or colledge,"
later named for John Harvard 18

12 THE MASSACHUSETTS GENERAL COURT requires the elementary
education of children 20

13 SAUGUS IRON WORKS marks the beginning of American
industrial history 21

14 CHRISTMAS is banned 23

15 QUAKER MARY DYER is hanged on Boston Common 24

16 JOHN ELIOT translates the Bible into the Algonquian Indian
language 26

17 KING PHILIP of the Wampanoag rebels against English colonists 28

18 THE SALEM WITCH TRIALS begin 30

19 DURING A SMALLPOX EPIDEMIC, Rev. Cotton Mather urges
experimentation with inoculations 32

20 JONATHAN EDWARDS delivers a hellfire sermon and ignites the
"Great Awakening" 34

21 JAMES OTIS DECLARES, "Taxation without representation
is tyranny" 36

22 THE SUGAR ACT and the Stamp Act arouse antiroyalist sentiments 37

23 JOHN SINGLETON COPLEY submits a portrait for exhibition at the Royal Academy in London 39

24 BRITISH TROOPS stationed in Boston fire on a mob, killing five men 41

25 PHILLIS WHEATLEY publishes the first book by an African American poet 43

26 BOSTONIANS PROTEST a tax on tea by throwing a shipment into Boston Harbor 44

27 PAUL REVERE AND OTHER RIDERS warn colonists that British regulars are marching on Concord 46

28 THE REVOLUTIONARY WAR begins in Lexington and Concord 47

29 DR. JOSEPH WARREN dies in the Battle of Bunker Hill 49

30 THE HANNAH receives its wartime commission from Gen. George Washington 51

31 BRITISH REDCOATS evacuate Boston 52

32 JOHN ADAMS drafts the Massachusetts Constitution 54

33 THE EMPRESS OF CHINA leaves Boston, beginning the China trade 56

34 DANIEL SHAYS leads a revolt against the state and federal governments 57

35 CHARLES BULFINCH supervises construction of the Massachusetts State House 59

36 JOHN ADAMS is elected second president of the United States 61

37 THE "GERRYMANDER" appears in a political cartoon condemning a redistricting plan 64

38 THE U.S. FRIGATE CONSTITUTION earns its nickname "Old Ironsides" 65

39 THE AMERICAN INDUSTRIAL REVOLUTION begins with steam-powered looms in Waltham 67

40 CAPT. HENRY HALL of Cape Cod begins commercial cranberry cultivation 70

41 MAINE is separated from Massachusetts in the Missouri Compromise 72

42 THE ESSEX is struck by a large sperm whale and sunk 74

43 UNITARIANISM, first organized in Boston, becomes the
unofficial religion of Boston Brahmins 75

44 THE FIRST COMMERCIAL RAILROAD hauls granite blocks
for the Bunker Hill Monument 77

45 DR. SAMUEL GRIDLEY HOWE opens the first school for the blind
in the country 79

46 WILLIAM LLOYD GARRISON begins publishing the
abolitionist journal *The Liberator* 81

47 MOUNT AUBURN CEMETERY, the nation's first "garden
cemetery," opens in Cambridge 83

48 HORACE MANN oversees creation of the first state board
of education 85

49 MARY LYON founds Mount Holyoke College, the nation's first
college for women 87

50 MARGARET FULLER is appointed editor of *The Dial*, a new
journal of transcendental thought 89

51 GEORGE AND SOPHIA RIPLEY create the Brook Farm
Institute of Agriculture and Education 91

52 FREDERICK DOUGLASS, an escaped slave, gives his first
public speech on Nantucket 93

53 HENRY DAVID THOREAU begins living at Walden Pond 95

54 THE FIRST OPERATION under anesthesia is
performed at Massachusetts General Hospital 97

55 THE FIRST NATIONAL WOMAN'S RIGHTS CONVENTION
convenes in Worcester 100

56 RUNAWAY SLAVE ANTHONY BURNS is captured in Boston
under the Fugitive Slave Act 101

57 THE FILLING of the Back Bay begins 103

58 MILTON BRADLEY publishes a board game, "The Checkered
Game of Life" 106

59 COL. ROBERT GOULD SHAW leads the nation's first African
American regiment 107

60 W. E. B. DUBOIS is born in Great Barrington 109

61 LOUISA MAY ALCOTT of Concord publishes *Little Women* 111

62 FIRE sweeps through downtown Boston 113

63 HARVARD AND MCGILL face off in "Boston football" 115

64 MARY BAKER EDDY founds Christian Science   *116*

65 ALEXANDER GRAHAM BELL, working in a Boston
garret, invents the telephone   *118*

66 THE NEW ENGLAND SOCIETY for the Suppression of Vice
is established   *120*

67 FREDERICK LAW OLMSTED begins work on the "Emerald
Necklace"   *121*

68 EMILY DICKINSON dies at the family home in Amherst   *123*

69 JAMES NAISMITH invents the game of basketball, in Springfield   *125*

70 LIZZIE BORDEN takes an ax   *127*

71 IN SPRINGFIELD, Frank Duryea test-drives the first American
gasoline-powered automobile   *129*

72 JOHN MCDERMOTT wins the first Boston Marathon   *131*

73 THE FIRST SUBWAY in America opens at Park Street Under   *133*

74 THE BOSTON PILGRIMS face the Pittsburgh Pirates in the
first World Series   *134*

75 THE "BREAD AND ROSES" STRIKE hits Lawrence's textile mills   *136*

76 PRESIDENT WOODROW WILSON nominates Boston attorney
Louis Brandeis to the U.S. Supreme Court   *138*

77 A TANK holding 2 million gallons of molasses bursts in the
North End   *141*

78 THE BOSTON POLICE STRIKE gains Gov. Calvin Coolidge
national prominence   *142*

79 HIS SHORT-LIVED financial empire in ruins, Charles Ponzi
of Boston is arrested for fraud   *144*

80 THE BOSTON RED SOX sell Babe Ruth to the New York
Yankees   *146*

81 IN AUBURN, Robert Goddard launches the first liquid-fuel
rocket   *148*

82 NICOLA SACCO AND BARTOLOMEO VANZETTI are executed   *149*

83 THE GREAT HURRICANE hits, costing millions in damages   *151*

84 THE SWIFT RIVER VALLEY is flooded to create the
world's largest man-made source of water   *152*

85 TED WILLIAMS bats .406   *154*

86 THE COCOANUT GROVE nightclub fire kills 492   *155*

87 THE COMPUTER AGE dawns in Cambridge laboratories   *157*

88 UNDER INDICTMENT for mail fraud, James Michael Curley
is reelected mayor of Boston   *158*

89 A HOLDUP of a Brink's armored car nets Boston thieves
$2.7 million   *160*

90 THE WORLD'S FIRST successful human kidney transplant
operation is performed   *162*

91 MALCOLM X opens Muhammad's Mosque II   *164*

92 THE BASIS for a female contraceptive is discovered at the
Worcester Foundation for Experimental Biology   *166*

93 MASSACHUSETTS SEN. JOHN FITZGERALD KENNEDY
is elected thirty-fifth U.S. president   *168*

94 THE "BOSTON STRANGLER" begins a twenty-one-month
spree of rape and murder   *170*

95 RAY TOMLINSON, a scientist in Cambridge, sends the
first e-mail message   *172*

96 NIXON 49, AMERICA 1—Massachusetts is the only state
to vote for George McGovern   *174*

97 A PHOTOGRAPH of an antibusing demonstration wins the
Pulitzer Prize   *175*

98 THIEVES REMOVE paintings worth $200 million from the
Isabella Stewart Gardner Museum   *177*

99 HIJACKERS SEIZE a pair of airliners bound from Boston to
Los Angeles   *179*

100 THE MODERN WORLD'S largest and most costly public works
project, "The Big Dig," ends   *181*

101 MASSACHUSETTS is home to World Series and Super Bowl
winners   *183*

BIBLIOGRAPHY   *185*

INDEX   *190*

Acknowledgments

PUNDITS LIKE TO SAY that Americans no longer know their history or have genuine interest in events older than a week ago. In my work on this book—and on its predecessor, *The Massachusetts Legacy* (Adams Media, 1995), I was struck by the great attachment so many citizens in the state feel for their local history. From Boston to the Berkshires, the people of Massachusetts shared their knowledge of the past with me freely.

For invaluable research assistance, I owe a debt—in some cases, now ten years old—to librarians and staff at the Boston Public Library and Brookline Public Library; Christine Peterson, branch librarian, Jane Bickford, adult librarian, and the staff of the West Roxbury Branch of the Boston Public Library; Philip S. Bergen, librarian, Bostonian Society; Virginia H. Smith, reference librarian, Massachusetts Historical Society; Richard Johnson, The Sports Museum of New England; Richard J. Wolfe, curator of rare books and manuscripts, Harvard Medical School Library; Lisa Tuite and Kathleen Hennrikus, Boston Globe Library; Carolyn M. Kemmett, Unitarian Universalist Association of Congregations; Sylvia Watts McKinney, Museum of Afro-American History/African Meeting House; George Sanborn, State Transportation Library; Nancy Gaudette, librarian, Worcester Room, Worcester Public Library; Malcolm J. Flynn, Boston Latin School; Nantucket Chamber of Commerce; and Nancy Heywood, James Duncan Phillips Library, Essex Institute.

For their personal assistance, thanks to Kevin McCaffrey, Mount Holyoke College; Janet Heywood, Friends of Mount Auburn Cemetery; Alan Banks, park ranger, Frederick Law Olmsted National Historic Site; Frances Gagnon, Springfield Historical Commission; Robin Jonathan Deutsch, Naismith Memorial Basketball Hall of Fame; Chris Phillips, Ocean Spray Cranberries; Jeanne Blum Kissane, Worcester Foundation; Gloria Greis, Peabody Museum of Archaeology and Ethnology; and Thomas Hutchinson, NYNEX.

For providing me with their publications and materials of historical interest, thanks to the Saugus Iron Works National Historic Site; Perkins School for the Blind; Quincy Historical Society; Immigrant City Archives, Lawrence; and Old Dartmouth Historical Society Whaling Museum, New Bedford.

Preface

GEORGIA HAS SWEET PEACHES, Florida has juicy oranges, Kansas has golden wheat. In Massachusetts, the bumper crop is history.

The Commonwealth of Massachusetts, as it is officially known, is largely undistinguished by geography. Mount Greylock, its highest point, rises only 3,487 feet. At 10,555 square miles, Massachusetts ranks forty-fourth of the fifty states in area. Six and a half million people live in Massachusetts, which places it as the thirteenth most populous state, according to the 2000 federal census.

Massachusetts stands out, nevertheless, for its ongoing contribution to the life of the nation. In politics and social reform, science and medicine, education, the arts, sports, and many other fields, Massachusetts has given the nation and the world a disproportionate share of landmark events and historic achievements. Identifying 101 of these events, this book offers a short course in the history of this great state.

Certainly, the American character was indelibly shaped by the first European settlers of Massachusetts. The Pilgrims and the Puritans imparted to their descendants a rigorous work ethic; a genuine respect for education and self-improvement; and a system of citizen government that forms the foundation of our national democracy. Self-righteous and suspicious, frequently even intolerant, the residents of the Bible commonwealth also bequeathed us the blue law and the witch trial.

Anyone born or raised in Massachusetts inevitably acquires a native pride in the role played by the commonwealth's citizens in the American Revolution. Citizens of Lexington and Concord, Bunker Hill and Dorchester Heights can remain justifiably proud two centuries after those names were first enrolled in the ledger of historic places. But the Massachusetts legacy is not confined to the days of powdered wigs and buckled shoes.

Throughout the nineteenth century, Massachusetts led the country to expand its definition of liberty. The constitution of the commonwealth of Massachusetts, drafted by John Adams in 1780, included a Bill of Rights, and stated unequivocally, "All men are born free and equal." This was quickly interpreted as a bar to slavery. In Boston, abolitionists such as William Lloyd Garrison provided escaped slave Frederick Douglass with a platform for his thundering denunciations of the South's "peculiar institution." Robert Gould Shaw and men of the African American 54th Massachusetts Regiment ultimately gave their lives on a Civil War battlefield for emancipation.

Massachusetts women also distinguished themselves. Margaret Fuller served as editor of the influential transcendentalist publication *The Dial*; novelist Louisa May Alcott created the enduring characters in *Little Women*; Mary Baker Eddy founded Christian Science.

Twentieth-century events have had far-reaching effects. The launch of Robert Goddard's rocket, on a farm just outside Worcester, was the first small step toward exploration of the solar system. The election of John Fitzgerald Kennedy as the U.S. president created a Massachusetts political dynasty to rival the Adams family. The birth control pill and a successful method for organ transplants have shaped the destinies of countless men and women.

I hope that *Massachusetts 101* contributes to my native Commonwealth—and to the global common wealth, too—if only by simply laying out for everyone the state's remarkable history and thus encouraging further examination and inquiry. Served in bite-sized pieces, my book is only a tasting menu of the annals of Massachusetts, but I count on the experience to be pleasant enough to whet the reader's appetite for more.

Christopher Kenneally
Boston, March 2005

Massachusetts

OFFICIAL NAME: Commonwealth of Massachusetts.

ORIGIN OF NAME: From Algonqian, for "large hill place."

ADMITTED TO STATEHOOD: February 6, 1788 (sixth).

CAPITAL: Boston (founded 1630).

MOTTO: Ense Petit Placidam Sub Libertate Quietem
(By the Sword We Seek Peace, but Peace Only under Liberty).

AREA: 10,555 square miles (44th of 50 states).

LONGITUDE/LATITUDE: 72°W/42° 30'N.

GEOGRAPHIC CENTER: Worcester, north part of city.

LENGTH: 190 miles.

WIDTH: 50 miles.

HIGHEST POINT: Mt. Greylock (3,487 feet).

MEAN ELEVATION: 500 feet.

POPULATION: 6,349,097 (2000 census; 13th largest).

HIGHEST/LOWEST RECORDED TEMPERATURE: 107°F, August 2, 1975,
at Chester and New Bedford: -35°F, January 12, 1981, at Chester.

1

Massachusetts reemerges as the Pleistocene ice sheet retreats.

A MOOSE BENT ITS ANTLERED HEAD AND SIPPED from a pond's soggy bank. Overhead, the sun shone and warmed the earth. The air temperature rose throughout the day, and life stirred everywhere. Deep in the pine woods, ice melted and dampened the forest floor, and patches of crusted snow lingered. The long winter of the last Pleistocene Ice Age was finally over.

No one knows for sure exactly when, but sometime between fifteen thousand and ten thousand years ago, Massachusetts and the rest of North America reemerged from under an ice sheet that had covered the land like the stone lid on a tomb. The landscape was resurrected and reinvigorated. Cranberry shrubs and mussels infiltrated its tidal marshes. Alewife and shad teemed in its pristine rivers. Deer grazed and bear hunted in its dense forests.

At its heaviest, the ice sheet rose nearly two miles high and weighed billions of tons. It reached as far south as the Missouri and Ohio river valleys. All of New England was buried, along with New York State and northern Pennsylvania. The massive ice sheet was not snowy white but dingy gray. When it descended from the north, the ice scraped across the surface of the earth like the blade of an awesome plow. The force carried off everything in its path—soil, stones, and boulders, down to the bedrock.

As it groaned forward, the ice sheet sculpted hills and rounded mountains; it etched deep grooves in exposed rock; and it sunk the earth where it was soft, like an artist's thumb pressing into clay. Without the ice sheet to shape it, Massachusetts as we know it would not exist. The history of the commonwealth can conceivably be traced to the formation of our planet 4.7 billion years ago, but Massachusetts before the Ice Age would be unrecognizable.

More than 200 million years ago, theropod beasts measuring fifty feet from head to tail roamed the mud that would later become the Connecticut River valley. Other, smaller dinosaurs—only about as large as a human being—shared the valley mud and the luxuriant tropical vegetation. Long after dinosaurs disappeared, the earth swung wildly between chilly periods of "glaciation," some lasting millions of years, and relatively shorter warming periods or "interglacials." Whatever tall mountains and fuming volcanoes provided backdrop for the age of the theropods, all have vanished under the unstoppable scouring action of advancing and retreating ice sheets.

When the most recent "interglacial" period began 15,000 years ago, the earth once more started to warm. The endangered ice sheet shrank back again toward the North Pole. Where chips of ice were trapped in depressed pockets of earth, they melted into pools, ponds, and lakes. As it retreated, the thawing glacier scattered a rubble of sand, rocks, and boulders. Where its gritty litter was piled hundreds of feet high, drumlins and moraines formed. The landscape of Massachusetts as we know it was created.

2

10,000–1500 BCE

Paleo-Indian hunters settle in Massachusetts.

AT LAST, A NAMELESS BAND OF PALEO-INDIAN hunters crossed an imaginary line that today marks a border of the commonwealth. They were the first human beings to set foot in Massachusetts. A tribe of rugged nomads, they searched the tundra for food. These first people were not alone. Caribou, mastodon, and mammoth roamed the land with them. The Paleo-Indians stalked these animals relentlessly. They dined on the great beasts' flesh, wore their thick skins for clothing, and from their bones fashioned weapons and crude tools.

When the ice sheet was entirely melted and all the heavy Pleistocene animals were extinct, the cultures that thrived in such an environment vanished, too. New England's Paleo-Indian population was probably never more than twenty-five thousand, and they left behind little evidence of their existence. At Bull Brook, near Ipswich, and at archaeological sites throughout the Connecticut River Valley of Massachusetts, Paleo-Indian remains include burned bones, knives, drills, and their distinctive fluted spear points.

The ancient weapons-making techniques worked reasonably well. Extremely difficult to make and requiring painstaking carving work, fluted projectiles were designed to hold a spear point securely to a long wooden shaft. One theory on the relatively sudden disappearance of Paleo-Indians suggests that they may have hunted themselves out of existence by systematically killing off their food source in great orgies of bloodletting and feasting.

By 8000 BCE, forests had replaced tundra in Massachusetts. The native peoples of the "Archaic Period" wandered less than their nomadic ancestors. They settled into hunting territories where they fished and gathered wild strawberries and other fruits. These early inhabitants ate clam chowder seasoned with artichokes, and porridge made from ground nuts and wild corn mixed with milk and butter. They roasted turkey and boiled bear meat.

The descendants of the Archaic Period and the Algonquians, who arrived in Massachusetts after 2000 BCE, transformed the landscape over the passing generations. To clear land for the cultivation of vegetables, they girdled trees to kill them and they burned the underbrush. With a high canopy overhead and open ground before them, they hunted deer with ease.

Seven native Indian tribes existed in what is now Massachusetts at the time of contact with Europeans: the Wampanoag; the Nauset; the Pennacook; the Nipmuc; the Pocumtuc; the Mohican; and the Massachusett, "the people of the Great Blue Hill," who lived on a crescent of land that curved around Boston Harbor from Salem to Braintree.

3

Bartholomew Gosnold explores the Massachusetts coast and names Cape Cod.

IN THE CHAMBER OF THE MASSACHUSETTS HOUSE of Representatives, an unusual totem hangs in the east gallery opposite the Speaker's chair. The "Sacred Cod," carved from a single block of pine, is an enduring legacy of the commonwealth's first industry and a reminder of the role cod once played as a powerful lure for Europeans to settle in Massachusetts.

In 1497 and 1498, Venetian-born explorer John Cabot sailed from Newfoundland to the waters off New England now known as Georges Bank, making him the first documented European to view the Massachusetts shore. Cabot reported that the cod were so plentiful, his men pulled the fish from the sea in baskets. Not long afterward, Breton, Basque, and Portuguese fishermen arrived to profit from such an easy catch.

In 1524, Giovanni da Verrazano of Florence sailed from Florida to Newfoundland in a fruitless search for the Northwest Passage leading to China and India. He stopped at Narragansett Bay for two weeks and explored inland, probably along the Taunton River. The local country, wrote the explorer to his French sponsors, "we found as pleasing as it can be to narrate. . . . The fields are from twenty-five to thirty leagues [seventy-five to ninety miles] wide, open and devoid of every impediment of trees, of such fertility that any seed in them would produce the best crops."

By 1578, at least four hundred European fishing vessels crowded Georges Bank, Massachusetts Bay, and the surrounding seas. Sailors landed and traded with the native people but did not seriously attempt to establish permanent settlements. Eventually France, England, and even the Netherlands all made claims to what is now Massachusetts.

In the area around Massachusetts Bay, early maps showed a pointed tip of land. Profit-minded English merchants sent Bartholomew Gosnold there in 1602 in search of sassafras. The plant's root, when made into tea, was popular as a cure for the "French pox" and other Elizabethan afflictions. Verrazano's account of New England a century earlier had described abundant sources of sassafras, but Gosnold could find none of it.

On May 18, 1602, Bartholomew Gosnold and his crew entered what is now Provincetown Harbor. The men fished while at anchor and caught so much cod that they were forced to throw many back into the sea. Gosnold marked the spot "Cape Cod." On the same voyage, he also landed on a nearby island where wild grapes were abundant. He named the island Martha's Vineyard after his daughter.

When Samuel de Champlain mapped the area in 1607, he named the same hooked peninsula Cap Blanc for its white, sandy beaches. English power soon predominated in the region, however. Today no one remembers "Cap Blanc."

4 | 1614

Capt. John Smith maps the coastline between Cape Cod Bay and Penobscot.

POCAHONTAS—WHOM HE MET SEVEN YEARS earlier—may not have been on Capt. John Smith's mind as he cruised through Cape Cod Bay in 1614. Of more immediate concern was the poor condition of the navigation charts he had brought from England as well as the unreliable descriptions of the region he had studied. He dismissed these accounts and the accompanying maps as "so differing from any true proportion or resemblance of the Countrey as they did mee no more good than so much waste paper, though they cost me more."

What Smith saw with his experienced explorer's eye persuaded him that the area was worth visiting. He paused to trade with local tribes and went away enriched handsomely. "We got for trifles near 1100 Bever skinnes, 100 martin [skins], and neer as many others."

Throughout the 1614 voyage, the first of two he would make to the seas north of Virginia, Capt. Smith measured the water's depth; took note of dangerous sandbars and rocks; and finally, drew up "a Map from Point to Point, Ile to Ile and Harbour to Harbour." Two years later, at home, Smith published the results as "The Description of New England." The name stuck.

On his map, Smith recorded the native names for rivers and other features, but he cunningly turned the draft over for editing to Prince Charles (later King Charles I), a potential patron. The fifteen-year-old's suggestions for changes were inspired by the names of his own family as well as that of English geography. Among the prince's lasting substitutions were Plymouth; Cape Anna (Cape Ann); and the River Charles, which the son named for his father.

5

1620

The Mayflower, carrying the Pilgrims, arrives in Cape Cod Bay.

IN SEPTEMBER 1620, THE MAYFLOWER SAILED FROM Plymouth, England, with 102 passengers and crew. The passengers crowded aboard belonged to a strict Calvinist sect who had separated from the official Church of England and were severely persecuted for their beliefs.

After living for ten years in relative peace in Leyden, Holland, these "Separatists"—whom we call the Pilgrims—decided to resettle in America. They read with longing in Capt. Smith's "The Description of New England" of "many iles all planted with corne; groves, mulberries, salvage gardens and good harbours." Holding a charter from the Virginia Company of London, the Pilgrims planned to make a fresh start in an uncharted

portion of "the Northern Parts of Virginia," where they hoped to practice their religion freely.

September is hurricane season in the North Atlantic. Unhappily for the Pilgrims, storms pounded the *Mayflower*. Whether the stout ship was blown off course, as is commonly believed, or whether the Pilgrims sailed toward Cape Cod Bay purposefully (even surreptitiously) is a matter of continuing argument for historians.

On November 21, the *Mayflower* landed near what is now Provincetown Harbor. The view from the small ship at anchor off Cape Cod in late November made a frightening prospect. Those who stood on deck had endured a sixty-six-day sea voyage. They saw they would now be tested further.

"For summer being done, all things stand upon them with a weather-beaten face," wrote one passenger, William Bradford, a native of Yorkshire. "The whole country, full of woods and thickets, represented a wild and savage hue." Such terror proved too great for Dorothy Bradford, William's wife. She threw herself overboard and was drowned.

In a boat he shared with Capt. Myles Standish and other Pilgrim men, William Bradford made several visits to shore. These trips qualified as raids, for as Bradford wrote, the hungry Pilgrims came upon Indian stores of corn and "beans of various color, which they brought away, purposing to give them full satisfaction when they should meet with any of [the Indians]."

Aware that their position outside the limits of the Virginia Company's charter put them in a precarious situation with the royal authorities, the Pilgrims drew up a substitute patent for the one they had brought from England. In a brief "compact" of fewer than 250 words, the settlers declared their intentions. "We whose names are underwritten," runs the document, "do by these presents solemnly and mutually in the presence of God and one of another, covenant and combine our selves together into a Civil Body Politick for our better Ordering and Preservation."

The American tradition of self-government was thus born with the "Mayflower Compact."

6

1621

The Pilgrims celebrate the first Thanksgiving.

OF THE 102 PILGRIMS WHO SAILED FROM ENGLAND in September 1620, fifty were dead by the following May. Among the dead was John Carver, first governor of the Pilgrims, but mortality was especially high among women. William Bradford was chosen Carver's successor and would be reelected thirty times before his death in 1657.

In spring 1621, the colonists planted seeds they had brought from England as well as those taken from Indian stores. English peas and wheat withered mysteriously, but native corn and other local vegetables grew well in the Plymouth soil. From the sea, the Pilgrims fished the plentiful cod and bass. With their muskets, they shot all manner of waterfowl and wild turkey. In the deep woods, they hunted deer.

The English enjoyed the peaceful welcome they received from the Wampanoag Indians. Throughout the worst of the first winter, the native people kept a distance from their uninvited guests. Indians occasionally showed themselves, though only indirectly: When a group of laboring colonists left behind their tools to eat dinner, the valuable instruments had vanished before the workmen returned.

Finally, in March 1621, a lone Indian walked fearlessly into Plymouth. The intruder, Samoset, stunned the Pilgrims even further when he spoke to them in broken English. An Algonquian from Pemaquid Point, in Maine, he explained that he had learned the white man's language from English fishermen and often worked with them as a guide and interpreter. When he next visited Plymouth, Samoset brought other Indians with him, as well as the missing set of tools.

Among Samoset's companions that second day was Squanto, who is remembered not only for his command of English but also for showing the colonists how to use fish as a fertilizer in their fields. A Pawtuxet Indian kidnapped by English sailors in 1605, Squanto lived in England until 1614, when Capt. John Smith agreed to return him home. Almost as soon as Smith left Squanto ashore, though, the hapless Indian was kidnapped again by a captain in Smith's fleet, who sold him into slavery in Spain.

Squanto managed to find his way home again in 1619. To his horror, however, he discovered that the Pawtuxet (who occupied the land where the Pilgrims later established Plimoth Plantation) had been wiped out two years earlier by a plague. The last surviving member of his tribe was forced to take up with a nearby Wampanoag tribe led by Massasoit.

When the harvest was over and stores were prepared for winter, the Pilgrims decided to show gratitude to their God. They invited Massasoit and about ninety of his people to rejoice with them and share a feast. After the first such celebration in 1621, other days for public "thanksgiving" were similarly observed at Plymouth in 1623 and 1630.

"Thanksgiving" was not officially made a holiday in the commonwealth until a century later. In 1723, Massachusetts governor William Dummer recognized "the many Instances of the Divine Goodness in the course of the Year past." He issued a proclamation "to order and appoint that Thursday the Twenty-eighth of November Currant be solemnly Observed as a Day of Publick Thanksgiving."

In 1789, President George Washington proclaimed the first national Thanksgiving in America. The campaign to make Thanksgiving a permanent holiday began in Boston in 1827, when Sarah Josepha Hale, editor of *Ladies' Magazine*, took up the cause. In 1863 President Lincoln put "Thanksgiving" forever on the calendar.

7

1623

William Blackstone settles at Shawmut Peninsula, the future site of Boston.

REV. WILLIAM BLACKSTONE (SOMETIMES SPELLED Blaxton), 27, an ordained minister in the Anglican Church and a recent graduate of Emmanuel College, accompanied Capt. Robert Georges to Massachusetts Bay in 1623. The Georges expedition was intended to establish a colony based at Wessagusset, now called Weymouth. Blackstone was to be the settlement's assistant pastor.

As with so many other early attempts at colonies in North America, the Georges expedition is remembered only for being a failure. The surviving members limped home in 1624, happy to be leaving with their lives. Among those the Georges colonists left behind were several men daring enough to make their solitary ways in the wilderness: Samuel Maverick, a trader, went to what is now East Boston; David Thompson took to an island in Boston Harbor later named for him; and Rev. Blackstone purchased from the local Native Americans eight hundred acres of land on "Shawmut," a bulb-shaped peninsula that jutted into Massachusetts Bay.

From all accounts, William Blackstone took to Shawmut like Henry David Thoreau later took to Walden Pond. He had a library of two hundred books and was a skilled farmer who tended a garden and an apple orchard. His house, presumably a simple log cabin, was situated near a spring with a view of the Charles River from the west slope of Beacon Hill. Blackstone lived on peaceful terms with his Indian neighbors. Though he remained a minister, Blackstone made no attempt to preach to them or otherwise save their souls.

In 1630, however, the idyll Blackstone enjoyed was shattered when a fleet of English boats sailed into waters surrounding the Shawmut peninsula. If he did not notice from his own hilltop lookout, then he learned the news from his watchful friends among the local Indians. Settlers began to build new homes in Charlestown on land across a narrow channel from Shawmut. Too late, though, they realized that their chosen site had no reliable source of fresh water.

Shawmut's solitary dweller emerged to help the newcomers. Blackstone told the thirsty Puritans about his clear spring, and they accepted a generous offer to resettle on his land. The Puritans were grateful enough to their benefactor: In appreciation for his actions, they graciously made him a member of their church and "gave" him fifty acres of his own land.

As he had grown weary of "the Lord Bishops" in England, William Blackstone soon grew tired of "the Lord Brethren." Preferring his own company, he sold his remaining land for £30, purchased a herd of cattle, and packed his books.

As he had done in 1624, Blackstone wandered blindly into the wilderness again. He made a new settlement by a river, now called the Blackstone River, near the present-day border with Rhode Island. The first citizen of Boston returned from his "Study Hill" only once, twenty years later, when he courted and married Mary Stephenson, a widow with a sixteen-year-old daughter. When Blackstone charged into town riding on the back of a bull, he found that the land where he had once planted his vegetables and orchard had become Boston Common, which later became the first public park in America.

8

John Winthrop leads Puritan ships into Massachusetts Bay.

A FLEET OF PURITAN SHIPS SAILED FROM ENGLAND in March 1630, at what was then celebrated as the start of a new year. John Winthrop, recently elected governor of the Massachusetts Bay Company, commanded the fleet's flagship, *Arbella*. During a three-month voyage, the former lawyer and country squire began a journal in which he compared himself to Moses leading a new Exodus.

In England, Winthrops were prosperous members of the gentry and owned a five-hundred-acre estate, Groton Manor, in Suffolk. In 1603, fifteen-year-old John Winthrop attended Trinity College, Cambridge, but he left his studies in 1605 to wed Mary Forth, the first of his four wives. Later he became a justice of the peace, and he was admitted to the bar in 1628. From an early age, Winthrop had been keenly religious. As a devout Puritan, he eventually became convinced that God had chosen him a member of the Elect. In 1629, he was disbarred for his Puritan beliefs; that same year, he signed on with the Massachusetts Bay Company.

When Winthrop spotted a loophole in the company's royal charter, his fellow colonists were delighted: by virtue of a significant oversight, meetings of the "General Court" were not required to be held in England. If the charter were transferred to New England, Winthrop suggested, the General Court could hold its sessions there and be free from oversight by the Crown. The other Puritans gave his plan their support and voted him governor. He would serve the people of Massachusetts in that office for the greater part of his life.

The Puritan fleet, carrying approximately one thousand passengers altogether, first docked in June 1630, at Salem, where an advance guard led by John Endicott met them. They continued on to Charlestown, where they landed within sight of the Shawmut peninsula. In September the colonists

Grave of John Winthrop

JOHN WINTHROP 1588 – 1649
1ST GOVERNOR of MASSACHUSETTS
VINTHROP the YOUNGER 160
1ST GOVERNOR of CONNECTICUT
N. FITZ JOHN WINTHROP 16
GOVERNOR of CONNECTICUT
WAIT STILL WINTHROP 1
HIEF JUSTICE of MASSACHUSET
AM WINTHROP 1647 – 17

renamed William Blackstone's solitary settlement "Boston" after a town in Lincolnshire where many of them had previously lived.

In a contemporary portrait by the school of Sir Anthony Van Dyck, John Winthrop makes the archetypical Puritan figure with his neat beard, stiff accordion collar, and thin, arched eyebrows. A determined and humorless man who demanded from his peers and himself extraordinary self-discipline, Winthrop was also a fearless and inspiring leader who was deeply admired by his fellow colonists and even chastised by them for sometimes being too lenient. More than any other first-generation Puritan, he was the colony's moral center.

The settlers of Boston and Charlestown endured an exceptionally brutal winter in their first year. At least two hundred died from exposure, malnutrition, and disease before spring. Within twelve months, yet another one hundred sailed home to England. By the decade's end, however, more than fifteen thousand English settlers had made the "Great Migration" to Massachusetts.

9

Anne Hutchinson outrages Boston clergy.

FROM THE PERSPECTIVE OF THREE AND A HALF centuries, important religious disputes within the Puritan church appear greatly diminished. Arguments concerning the strict primacy of grace over works even verge on unintentional comedy to the contemporary mind, but these were hardly petty matters to the commonwealth's first citizens. Church and state were inseparable for them. A dispute in the former made for disturbing chaos in the latter.

When Anne Hutchinson began holding well-attended meetings in her Boston home in 1634, during which she challenged basic tenets of the prevailing Puritan orthodoxy, the authorities' response was quick and harsh.

A skilled nurse and midwife, Anne Marbury Hutchinson was raised in Lincolnshire, England. The daughter of an Anglican cleric who had overseen her thorough education, she was able to participate effortlessly in convoluted discussions of religious doctrine and to question established authority. In 1612, Anne, twenty-one, married William Hutchinson, a merchant. They would eventually have fifteen children.

In England, the Hutchinsons became followers of John Cotton, an Anglican minister with Puritan sympathies. When Cotton immigrated to the Massachusetts Bay Colony in 1634, the Hutchinsons went, too. Moving among mostly dour Puritan women, Anne Hutchinson immediately stood out both because of her education and because of what John Winthrop later called her "ready wit and bold spirit."

With the good wives of Boston gathered around her at her home, Hutchinson launched into pithy commentaries on the minister's Sunday sermons. She discussed "dark places of Scripture" and occasionally delivered a prophecy. At her most popular, Hutchinson attracted crowds of sixty to eighty men and women.

Statue of Anne Hutchinson, Boston

Hutchinson's most startling claim was that the voice of God spoke to her. This admission was considered a heresy among fundamentalist Puritans, who followed only the word of God written in the Bible. The sharp-tongued preacher's daughter made matters worse by declaring that a soul was to be saved by an infusion of grace, not by works. This suggestion deeply offended many, especially John Winthrop, who believed such a "Covenant of Grace" abrogated the moral responsibility implied in a "Covenant of Works."

Finally, when Hutchinson dared to suggest in 1636 that only two of Boston's ministers were qualified to preach (John Cotton, of course, as well as John Wheelwright, her brother-in-law), she was instantly labeled a revolutionary. In 1638, she was brought to trial before the General Court. Although she did not confess to any crime, Hutchinson did repeat that God spoke directly to her. Because of this alleged heresy, the court excommunicated her and banished her from the commonwealth.

Hutchinson first moved to Aquidneck Island, now a part of Rhode Island. Later still, she moved farther from the Puritans, into Dutch-controlled territory on Long Island Sound. John Winthrop dogged her at each step. When Hutchinson and her family were murdered by Indians in 1643, Winthrop detected the clear hand of divine retribution.

10

1635

The first public school in America, the Boston Latin School, is founded.

AUTOMOBILE BUMPER STICKERS FREQUENTLY exaggerate the truth, but not in the case of those for the Boston Latin School. "Sumus primi," the stickers declare in bold purple script—"We're number one!" Whatever the current fortunes of Latin's athletic teams or its students, the boast rings true in at least one sense: Boston Latin owns forever the title of the first public school founded in America.

In a region thick with costly private academies and exclusive boarding schools Boston Latin stands out as a free public school that offers rigorous college preparatory courses. All Boston schoolchildren are eligible to apply, and are admitted according to their academic merit. For generations, Latin's high standards have allowed hardworking students of every ethnic background to compete for spaces at prestigious colleges and universities once reserved to the wealthy. A large percentage of each year's graduating class is admitted to Harvard College. Latin remains a required course at the Latin School, and the classical education includes instruction in ancient Greek and ancient history.

A list of Latin School luminaries reads like a Who's Who in American history. A very abbreviated rendering of that four-century roster includes theologian Cotton Mather; architect Charles Bulfinch; Revolutionary War general Henry Knox; John Collins Warren, a founder of Massachusetts General Hospital; transcendentalist Ralph Waldo Emerson; abolitionist Wendell Phillips; philosopher George Santayana; ambassador Joseph P. Kennedy, Jr.; Boston Pops conductor Arthur Fiedler; composer Leonard Bernstein; and author Theodore White. Also among Boston Latin's graduates are five signers of the Declaration of Independence: John Hancock, Samuel Adams, Benjamin Franklin, Robert Treat Paine, and William Hooper.

Puritan Boston abounded in the sort of self-made type who considers education mostly in practical terms as a means to success. The country's oldest public school was created on April 13, 1635, by citizens attending "a Generall meeting upon publique notice." They voted to appoint Philemon Pormort "to become scholemaster for the teaching & nourtering of children" at what was first known as the Latin Grammar School.

Boston, then a five-year-old settlement on the Charles River, already was populated by many industrious college graduates from the English middle class. Naturally, these men (for only men were allowed to attend college) expected their sons to be likewise instructed in reading, writing, "cyphering," and spelling as well as in Greek and Latin. That there were also classes in religion goes without saying.

The Puritans recognized that learning was an end in itself, yet they were not prepared to face the consequences of a strictly free public education. The early Latin School curriculum was rigidly proscribed, and its disciplinary code promised harsh punishment for any offenders. Puritan leaders such as John Winthrop demanded conformity of thought and stifled debate.

Philemon Pormort, appointed first "master" of the Latin School, was quickly run out of his job for poor pedagogic conduct. With many other prominent Bostonians, he had taken the side of Anne Hutchinson in her divisive religious quarrel with the Puritan theocrats. In 1638 Pormort chose to leave Boston for the new settlement of Exeter, New Hampshire. The exiled schoolmaster did not establish Exeter Academy in revenge. That well-known private college preparatory school opened in 1781.

11 | 1636

The General Court establishes a "schoale or colledge" later named for John Harvard.

ON OCTOBER 25, 1636, THE SAME DAY IT PASSED legislation forbidding the sale of lace for garments except for "binding or small edging laces," the Massachusetts General Court also "agreed to give £200 towards a schoale or colledge, whereof £200 to bee paid the next yeare, and £200 when the worke is finished, and the next Court to appoint wheare and what building."

The Puritans' commitment to higher education was hardly trifling, since £400 represented almost one quarter of the Massachusetts Bay Colony's total tax levy in 1636.

In November 1637 the legislators chose "Newetowne," later renamed Cambridge, as the school's site. According to Samuel Eliot Morison, who wrote the definitive *History of Harvard University*, the English-born founders were very likely thinking of Oxford and the original Cambridge when they fixed on "Newetowne." They would have believed a college required a river and that its campus should be located well enough inland. They rejected without comment a proposal to locate it on a three-hundred-acre farm between Salem and Marblehead. By contrast with the future Harvard Yard, the Salem land abutted the rough sea.

This act of 1636 directly led to the founding of Harvard College in Cambridge, though its namesake had not even left England. A well-to-do member of the landed class, John Harvard, 29, was recently graduated from Emmanuel College, Cambridge, as an ordained clergyman and was newly married when he arrived in the colony in 1637.

In London the Harvard family owned several homes and a good deal of land. As a devout Puritan, however, Harvard chose to leave all that for the hardships of Massachusetts. Once settled, he was installed as an assistant to the local minister.

Meanwhile, after three years of planning, the new college at Cambridge opened in the summer of 1638. Throughout that fateful summer, there were "signs and portents." In June an earthquake rumbled loud enough to remind John Winthrop of the "rattling of coaches in London." In August a hurricane lashed the Massachusetts shoreline and was felt particularly forcefully in Charlestown, where it toppled a windmill not far from the Harvard house.

No one knows for certain, but a curious John Harvard may have visited the new campus and formed the kernel of a resolution that would earn him enduring fame. When he succumbed to consumption on September 14, 1638, Harvard had made his deathbed wish clear to several witnesses: He wanted "to give one half of his Estate (about £1,700) toward the erection of a Colledge and all his Library." The next spring, the General Court resolved to name the first Massachusetts college in his honor.

Little else is known about John Harvard, and no contemporary likeness of him survives. The model for Daniel Chester French's statue in Harvard Yard was not Harvard at all, but a member of the Class of 1882, Sherman Hoar.

12

The Massachusetts General Court requires the elementary education of children.

FROM THE EARLIEST DAYS, PUBLIC EDUCATION IN America was infused with social goals. A law passed by the Massachusetts General Court on April 14, 1642, noted "the great neglect of many parents and masters in training their children in learning and labor and other implyments which may be profitable to the common wealth."

The Puritans envisioned public schools as a remedy for ignorance and moral degeneracy. This was a progressive vision, but within limits. The first public school law issued in the English-speaking world mandated coeducation, but required "that boys and girls be not suffered to converse together, so as may occasion any wanton, dishonest or immodest behavior." Puritan schools were also charged to prepare students to "read and understand the principles of religion and the capital lawes of the country."

Five years later the Massachusetts legislature took further steps toward establishing a public education system. A 1674 law required towns of fifty families to "appoint a master to teach all such children as shall resort to him to write & reade." In addition, towns of a hundred families were required to establish a "grammar" school to prepare students for college.

The Puritans, for obvious reasons, emphasized ecclesiastical instruction over other subjects. They believed that a Christian congregation should be able to read the Scriptures in their own tongue, and that therefore a primary education should teach children to read and write English. A preamble to the 1642 school law noted that "ye ould deluder, Satan [wanted] to keepe men from the knowledge of ye Scriptures by keeping ym in an unknown tongue." Before this, schools in England and elsewhere were usually conducted in Latin and other classical languages.

1646

Saugus Iron Works marks the beginning of American industrial history.

THE RAW MATERIALS NECESSARY TO PRODUCE IRON were easily obtained in the Massachusetts Bay Colony at the middle of the seventeenth century. Seemingly endless forests would provide charcoal for furnaces and lumber for the mills. Surging rivers would deliver energy to turn waterwheels and operate other primitive machinery. There was iron ore in abundance and, most important, the first successful miners could expect a monopoly (similar to holding a patent) on manufacturing rights for twenty-one years. There was only one problem. No one in Massachusetts knew the first thing about how to run an iron works.

John Winthrop, the son of the governor, decided to solve the dilemma. The younger Winthrop was a canny businessman with a background in metallurgy gained at Trinity College, Dublin. He understood that English capital was necessary if the colonists were to open an iron works from scratch. In 1641 he sailed from Boston to England with iron ore samples and the General Court's endorsement.

Winthrop scoured London for investors to join the proposed "Company of Undertakers of the Iron Works in New England." Not surprisingly, he was most successful with the city's Puritans. Winthrop also hoped to entice skilled and unskilled workers to follow him back to Boston. He managed to sign several skilled workers for the venture, but only a few of them were devout Puritans. Regrettably, they presented a menace to Boston's moral probity.

For his unskilled laborers, Winthrop took home an especially unsavory group. John Becx, a shareholder in the investment company, purchased the freedom of sixty Scots after they were captured by Cromwell's army and imprisoned. The hapless Scots now became the indentured servants of the Massachusetts Puritans, which must have seemed an attractive alternative to rotting in an English prison.

Saugus Iron Works

Known as Hammersmith, Winthrop's iron works was opened at a site on the Saugus River in 1646. Miners collected ore from nearby ponds and swamps. The ore and flux, a substance that separates iron from the raw ore, were dumped with heaps of charcoal into an enormous furnace. Molten iron then collected in crucibles until workers let it run into furrows dug in sand, where the iron formed bars. The bars were shaped into tools and nails. Molten iron was also cast in molds as pots, kettles, and iron "firebacks" for hearths.

Massachusetts court records show that many of the first ironworkers were frequent visitors to Puritan courtrooms. They were usually tried on charges of drunkenness, wife-beating, foul speech, and nonattendance at church. Others married into Puritan families and adopted more sober ways.

The iron works at Saugus operated until 1668, when it was shut down under the burden of mounting debts. The Saugus workers dispersed throughout the English colonies, where their knowledge and experience helped fuel the growth of American industry.

14

Christmas is banned.

THE "BLUE LAWS" OF MASSACHUSETTS, CONNECTICUT, and other Puritan-ruled colonies followed prescriptions set out in the Bible for the observance of the Sabbath. Ordinary work was banned as well as buying and selling goods, traveling, public entertainment, and any sports. The most notorious of the blue laws was written in the painstakingly direct, plain style favored by Puritan legislators: "Whosoever shall be found observing any such day as Christmas or the like, either by for-bearing of labour, feasting or in any other way . . . every such person so offending shall pay for every such offense five shillings, as a fine to the country."

In the English colonies of the Puritan era, biblical law allowed the church to govern through the instrument of a secular state. Blue laws included such now unconstitutional rules of justice as "the judges shall determine controversies without a jury" and "a wife shall be good evidence against her husband." In addition, town selectmen who had determined any children in their community to be "ignorant" were given authority to "take them from their parents and put them into better hands, at the expense of their parents."

Sanctions on Christmas celebrations were lifted as early as 1681, when second-generation Puritans began to assume political control across the commonwealth. Puritan sons and daughters proved not quite so strict as their fathers and mothers in matters of religious observance.

15

1660

Quaker Mary Dyer is hanged on Boston Common.

THE PURITANS MAY NOT HAVE ALLOWED THEATER or other entertainments in their midst, but for sheer spectacle they could always take a stroll through the Boston Common. Passersby might linger there at the stocks and pillory, the whipping post, and the gallows to enjoy thrilling demonstrations of the efficacy of leather straps, hot irons, and the noose.

Contemporary accounts of public punishments in seventeenth-century Boston can read like the diary entries of the Marquis de Sade. William Brend, described as "a man of years," went to the whipping post and received "One Hundred and Seventeen Blows with a pitch'd rope so that his Flesh was beaten Black and as into a Gelly." Women offenders were "stripped naked [and] beaten with whips of threefold knotted cord until the blood ran down their bare backs and breasts." Luckier convicts were branded, mutilated, or simply shackled and left to starve.

Among crimes thought deserving of hanging was being a practicing member of the Society of Friends. Known derisively for their pacifism as "Quakers," the Friends were denounced in 1656 by the Massachusetts General Court as a "cursed sect" who were "open blasphemers, open seducers from the Glorious Trinity . . . and from the Holy Scriptures as the rule of life, open enemies of government itself."

One of those who successfully pushed for passage of a law banishing Quakers was the Reverend John Norton, a pastor of Boston's First Church. Barely able to contain himself, Norton vented his righteous anger: "I would carry fire in one hand and fagots [kindling wood] in the other to burn all the Quakers in the world," he thundered. "Hang them or else." The law specified that any banished Quaker would be put to death if he or she dared return.

Surprisingly, the Puritans and Quakers had much in common. Both groups sought to restore simplicity to Christian practices. Both also denied the importance of sacraments and formal prayer. Like Anne Hutchinson and the "Antinomians," who preached the power of grace over the power of "works" to liberate the soul, Quakers professed a primary reliance on an "inner light" rather than obedience to law or Scripture. This position put Massachusetts Quakers in open conflict with the reigning Puritan theocracy.

Indeed, Mary Dyer, a "comely and grave matron," first drew the attention of the Puritans when she took Anne Hutchinson's side against them in 1635. Later, rumors circulated that Dyer had delivered a stillborn "monster," with a witch acting as midwife. She finally left Massachusetts with Hutchinson in 1638 and lived quietly in the more tolerant Rhode Island for almost twenty years.

In 1657, Mary Dyer provoked the Puritans when she traveled back to Boston; she was immediately arrested. The authorities released her into her husband's custody upon his promise that he would not let her speak while in Massachusetts. Defiantly, Dyer returned to Boston two years later to visit several Quaker prisoners, including an eleven-year-old girl. A Puritan court now formally banished her and made aware its intention to hang her if she dared come back a third time, which the irrepressible Quaker did the following month.

On October 27, 1659, Mary Dyer approached the gallows on Boston Common with two other condemned Quakers, William Robinson and Marmaduke Stephenson, at her side. She was bound and made to watch the men die first. With a handkerchief loaned from an attending minister, the executioner covered the woman's face before a reprieve—prepared in advance and given to Dyer on account of her sex—was read to dramatic effect. Nevertheless, Mary Dyer could not be denied her martyrdom. She returned to Boston the next year and was hanged June 1, 1660. "I have been in paradise several days" were her last words.

16

John Eliot translates the Bible into the Algonquian Indian language.

WHEN HE GRADUATED FROM JESUS COLLEGE, Cambridge University, in 1662, eighteen-year-old John Eliot had been thoroughly trained in written and spoken Latin, Greek, and Hebrew as well as the Bible, ancient history, logic, and public declamation. Cambridge dons had provided Eliot, the son of a prosperous yeoman landholder in Hertfordshire and Essex, England, with the sort of rigorous education common in Europe since the Middle Ages. The various skills he acquired—some obviously useful, others less apparently so—served Eliot well in the wilderness of Massachusetts.

In 1625 Eliot was ordained in the official Church of England. Over the next five years, however, the young minister drifted into the Puritan camp, where his piety and intellectual achievements were highly valued. In 1631 he sailed for the Bay Colony just as persecution of "dissenters" like himself was reaching a high pitch in England.

In the early seventeenth century, spreading the gospel was a busy line of work. Many Puritan colonists of Massachusetts Bay were determined to collect for God the souls of the country's native Indians. With unintentional irony, these Puritan preachers also thanked their God for the plague that decimated Massachusetts tribes living around Boston in the years immediately before its settlement. Puritan missionaries may have wanted Indian souls for conversion, but not so many that they couldn't properly handle them all.

As an evangelist, John Eliot took the challenge of preaching to the Indians one step farther than his colleagues. Rather than wait for the natives to learn English, which was the typical practice, the enterprising pastor of the First Church in Roxbury set out to master the native people's own language. To put it mildly, he started from scratch. The Algonquian tongue spoken in Massachusetts had as yet no articulated rules of grammar, no written texts, and no dictionary.

While philosophers and others strenuously sought to prove that Algonquian and all Indian languages were derived from Hebrew (based on a theory that one of the lost tribes of Israel had somehow managed to cross the Atlantic), Eliot boldly puzzled it all out. He carefully listened to and penetratingly questioned Cockenoe, a young Indian who worked in a Dorchester colonist's home and spoke fluent English. With Cockenoe as his source, Eliot discovered that Algonquian nouns were not divided by gender, as in many European languages, but by a distinction made between animate and inanimate objects. He also cataloged the many inflections possible in Algonquian and decoded multisyllabic word chains.

By 1653 Eliot had published a translation of the Book of Psalms, and in 1658 he told friends that his self-appointed task of translating the whole Bible was complete. From England, the Society for the Propagation of the Gospel provided financial assistance for the ambitious printing job. The New Testament appeared from the press of Samuel Green in Cambridge in 1661, and a complete edition of Old and New Testaments was published in 1663. It was the first Bible published in North America in any language.

Mamusse Wunneetupanatamwe Up-biblum God, begins the title page. *Naneeswe Nukkone Testament kah wonk Wusku Testament.*

During the long work of translation, Eliot found time to preach extensively and to establish more than a dozen "Praying Indian" towns. The first of these, Natick, was created in 1650 from a grant of land by Dedham. (Parts of this original Natick are now the separate towns of Wellesley, Sherborne, and Needham.) These settlements usually had a meetinghouse, a school, and a fort. The assimilated Indians lived in wigwams, farmed their own land, and chose their own leaders. In 1645, Eliot also founded the Roxbury Latin School, now located in West Roxbury.

John Eliot died in 1690 at the age of 86 and is remembered on his tomb as the "Apostle to the Indians."

17

King Philip of the Wampanoag rebels against English colonists.

WAMSUTTA AND METACOM, THE TWO SONS OF CHIEF Massasoit, visited Plymouth together in 1660 following their father's death. Wampanoag royal tradition demanded that the English settlers could not call the brothers by their given names. Accordingly, the colonists gave the pair names of kings from ancient Greek history: Wamsutta, the elder, became Alexander; Metacom, his younger brother, was rechristened Philip.

On their return home, Alexander died and Philip became the Wampanoag chief, or "sachem." The son was of an entirely different character than his peace-loving father. Philip resented the frequent summons he received to come to Plymouth. He greatly irritated the authorities by selling his land to whomever he pleased without their consent.

"King Philip" explained his reluctance to negotiate with the colonists as a matter of royal prerogative. "Your governor is but a subject of King Charles. I shall not treat with a subject," he said boldly. "I shall treat of peace only with the king, my brother. When he [Charles II] comes, I am ready."

Moving inexorably toward conflict with the English, King Philip sought to forge an alliance among New England tribes. He was successful, however, only in persuading the Pocumtuc, Narragansett, and Nipmuc to join him. When he finally went to war in 1675, Philip found himself nearly alone against the colonists, but he was "determined not to live until I have no country."

King Philip's War began ostensibly as a reaction to the trial and execution of three Wampanoag warriors who had murdered a fellow tribesman for informing on King Philip's plans. Wampanoags, Nipmucs, and Narragansetts raided numerous farms and settlements, including Swansea, Rehoboth, and Taunton.

The colonists' response was predictable and harsh. The English even turned against the assimilated tribes of "Praying Indians," whom, they feared, might join with Philip as allies. Native residents of Natick and Wamesit (now Tewksbury) were transported under harsh winter conditions to concentration camps on Long Island and Deer Island in Boston Harbor.

In July 1676 King Philip's wife and son were captured by English soldiers. "Now I am ready to die," the proud sachem declared.

When a fellow tribesman suggested that the Wampanoag should sue for peace, Philip gave his answer by executing the man instantly. He could not bring himself to surrender. This last rash act cost Philip dearly. The dead warrior's brother fled camp and informed the English where the Wampanoag sachem could be found.

A month later, Benjamin Church, who had doggedly pursued Philip across Rhode Island and southeastern Massachusetts, prepared for a dawn attack. The advantage of surprise was lost when a nervous colonist's gun discharged unexpectedly. In the confusion, Philip tried to escape but was hit by musket fire and mortally wounded. The chief's body was brutally quartered and the pieces hung in trees. A Pocasset tribesman named Alderman, who had fired the deadly shots, received Philip's hand as a memento. The colonists traveled to Plymouth with Philip's head, where it was left on display as a gruesome symbol of the white man's power.

In all, some twenty-five hundred colonists died in King Philip's War, along with at least an equal number of Indians. The rebellion was the most sustained outburst of native resentment ever seen in colonial New England.

18

1692

The Salem witch trials begin.

THE EXISTENCE OF DEMONS AND THE EFFICACY OF witchcraft were accepted as facts throughout the world in 1692. The Puritans of Salem Village (part of present-day Danvers) were certain of the devil's hand in every incident of evil they suffered, from petty misfortune to appalling tragedy. Witches and other agents of "the ould deluder" Satan delivered to the people of the commonwealth all manner of torments: deadly epidemics of smallpox; murderous raids by Indians; and ignorant children.

In 1648, Margaret Jones of Charlestown was the first person executed in Massachusetts for witchcraft. A practicing physician, Jones fell under suspicion of having a "malignant touch" after certain of her patients vomited or suffered violent seizures. Prison guards testified that they watched a little child run out of the witch's cell into another room, where the apparition vanished. Trial records described Jones as "very intemperate, lying notoriously and railing upon the jury and witnesses."

The magistrates and good people of Boston were later assured of the propriety of their verdict and sentence. On the same day and time that Margaret Jones went to the gallows, they learned, "there was a very great tempest at Connecticut, which blew down many trees." A thunderstorm was among the more substantial of the weird signs Beelzebub and his demons gave for their presence. More typical was "spectral evidence," which amounted simply to dreams, visions, and hallucinations. In court, testimony of the accused witch's "shape" making an appearance to its victim was the most notorious of such "evidence." Puritan magistrates took as doctrine that the devil could not assume the shape of an innocent person. Thus testimony that one's "shape" had visited the victim's bedroom was considered irrefutable.

In the winter of 1692, Elizabeth Parris, nine-year-old daughter of the Reverend Samuel Parris, and Abigail Williams, her eleven-year-old cousin,

Danvers Witch Memorial

IN MEMORY OF THOSE INNOCENTS
WHO DIED DURING THE
SALEM VILLAGE WITCHCRAFT HYSTERIA
OF 1692

began to have convulsions. The girls complained of a choking feeling in their throats and that they sometimes could not see or hear properly. An invisible hand was pinching them all over, they said, causing tiny marks to appear on their skin.

An unpopular minister with a notoriously cranky congregation, Rev. Parris was eaten with fear that he would fired from his poorly paid position. The children's behavior unnerved him still further. All winter, he insisted that the children reveal who or what was afflicting them.

Finally, the girls accused three women of spiritually torturing them: Tituba, a slave in the Parris household who was born in Barbados; Sarah Good, a nearly destitute woman with a reputation for being slovenly; and Sarah Osburne, a woman of property, until recently a widow, who was known for enjoying male company and who did not attend church services regularly. Under pressure, Tituba confessed: She had spoken with cats with wings and red rats who commanded her to serve them.

Now the tinderbox of Salem Village erupted, and an inferno spread across the commonwealth. By the end of September 1692, at least 150 people (including many children) were arrested, and 19 were hanged. Rebecca Nurse, an elderly mother who had raised eight children, was one of five witches hanged on Gallows Hill in July despite the pleadings of her family. Giles Corey, who had earlier testified against his wife, Martha, refused to enter a not guilty plea, thinking that this would save him from prosecution. To force him to plead, the sheriff led Corey to a field beside the Salem jail and, following English custom, began piling stones on the man's chest. Still refusing to plead, Corey was pressed to death. Before his chest collapsed under the weight, a resolute Corey managed to say, "More weight, more weight."

At last, in October, Massachusetts governor Sir William Phips threw out the validity of spectral evidence and halted further trials. Several magistrates insisted on continuing to hear witchcraft cases, but any convictions were swiftly set aside. Sense slowly returned to those in the commonwealth who, in the worlds of one judge, "had walked in clouds." January 15, 1697, was designated a day of repentance. The legislature annulled all the convictions, and in 1711 Massachusetts made restitution to the victims' families.

19

1721

During a smallpox epidemic, Rev. Cotton Mather urges experimentation with inoculations.

THE BRITISH VESSEL *SEAHORSE* ARRIVED AT BOSTON Harbor from the British West Indies in April 1721. Along with a cargo of sugar and other goods, the ship carried two slaves ill with contagious smallpox. In short order, a devastating epidemic began to spread throughout the city. Among the population of 11,000, nearly 6,000 people became infected with the disease, and 844 died.

At the height of the smallpox terror, Boston's wharves were all but deserted. Funeral bells rang continuously from church towers, and weary citizens complained about the depressing din. In Charlestown, the sexton was restricted to three funeral tolls daily so that the sick and their families might not be overly discouraged. The epidemic of 1721 proved to be the worst of its kind to hit Boston in the eighteenth century. Yet remarkably, it might have been even worse.

Before 1721, Boston's authorities relied on various methods of quarantine to isolate smallpox victims from the general population. A quarantine hospital was built on Spectacle Island in 1717. However, in an era when most physicians believed that disease was spread by bad air, the spread of smallpox was only slowed down by quarantines that were loosely observed. Even though the infected slaves aboard the *Seahorse* were brought to shore and confined, for example, the smallpox spread all the same.

Cotton Mather watched the epidemic with mounting anxiety. The respected if not especially well-liked minister of Boston's largest Puritan congregation, he somberly conducted funeral masses for those who died of smallpox. Mather also sought to calm his son, Samuel, whose roommate at Harvard had come down with the disease and died. Samuel himself showed no sign yet of having smallpox, though it was perhaps only a matter of time.

With his congregation and his own family in mind, Cotton Mather now gathered his courage. He feared the consequences of what he would say, but he feared more the consequences of silence. Boldly, Mather exhorted Boston physicians to begin a course of inoculation, something never before tried in the colonies. The minister, who wrote *The Wonders of the Invisible World*, a catalog of witchcraft and demonry, had learned of inoculation in British scientific and medical literature. In theory, inoculation initiated a mild form of a disease, one that the body was capable of resisting and that would leave an individual immune against other, more virulent strains of the same disease.

In addition, Mather had the fascinating testimony of an African slave, Onesimus, who told him how a tribal operation had miraculously left him immune to smallpox. Onesimus showed the curious Puritan a scar on his arm, a telltale sign of inoculation. The Puritans had often noted that their African-born slaves rarely fell ill with smallpox.

Three centuries ago, with scant evidence and no assurance of success, physicians hesitated to try inoculation. If the inoculations didn't work, they would inadvertently be helping to spread smallpox rather than providing immunity against it. Boston physicians chose to hedge their bets and stubbornly refused to follow Mather's advice.

One physician, however, broke ranks: Zabdiel Boylston of Muddy River (now Brookline). A survivor of smallpox in his infancy, Boylston inoculated his six-year-old son and two slaves with pus from a smallpox patient. He used a sharp toothpick and quill as his surgical instruments. All three patients subsequently had mild infections, but then they recovered and resisted further infection.

For a time, Dr. Boylston became a prisoner in his own home, unwilling to face the wrath of fearful neighbors and enraged colleagues. Still, the brave physician managed to inoculate nearly 250 people, only 6 of whom died from smallpox. In Roxbury and Cambridge, two doctors inoculated 36 others. Resistance to the procedure persisted, nevertheless. In November, a bomb broke through a window in Mather's house but failed to explode. "I'll inoculate you with this with a pox to you," read an attached note.

The vicious smallpox epidemic finally subsided in Boston the following spring.

20 | 1741

Jonathan Edwards delivers a hellfire sermon and ignites the "Great Awakening."

MASSACHUSETTS MINISTER JONATHAN EDWARDS had a speaking style known as "the preaching of terror."

"The God that holds you over the pit of hell, much as one holds a spider, or some loathsome insect, over the fire, abhors you, and is dreadfully provoked!" he roared to a presumably sweating Enfield congregation on July 8, 1741. "His wrath towards you burns like fire!"

That memorable image from "Sinners in the Hands of an Angry God" suggests that Jonathan Edwards was the quintessential preacher of "hellfire and brimstone" and a narrow-minded zealot. Instead, however, Edwards was a keen intellectual who was scrupulously well read in contemporary philosophy as well as the latest scientific discoveries. For all that knowledge, he firmly believed in the Puritan doctrine of predestination and the eternal torment of lost souls.

Edwards was born in Windsor, Connecticut, in 1703. At thirteen, he entered Yale College, where he studied divinity and taught for most of the next seven years. Influenced by British philosophers John Locke and Isaac Newton as much as by contemporary religious figures, Edwards gradually developed what he called a "rational account" of Christianity. In 1729 the twenty-six-year-old was appointed to the pulpit at Northampton, considered then the most important such post in New England outside of Boston.

In his sermons, Edwards deplored the colonists for what he saw as lax religious behavior. He condemned them for their increasing distance from God and for the growing belief in free will. Owing much to Edwards's effort, a revivalist movement known as the "Great Awakening" swept through New England and spread soon into other English colonies. Edwards delivered a series of sermons in November 1734 that led more than three hundred people to make professions of conversion, but it was not until 1740 when other preachers, specializing in "pathetical" or "emotional" sermons, set off nearby a hysterical round of mass conversions.

Hell, for Jonathan Edwards, was as real as anything could be. He did not make idle threats. Edwards spoke as plainly and convincingly as a journalist reporting from the scene of the latest famine or war. "Imagine yourself to be cast into a fiery oven, all of a glowing heat, or into the midst of a glowing brick-kiln, or of a great furnace, where your pain would be as much greater than that occasioned by accidentally touching a coal fire, as the heat is greater," Edwards said suggestively to his audience. Lying there in that oven, he added, there would be no end to the pain even "after millions of millions of ages."

Not everyone in the commonwealth found reason to admire Edwards and his ilk. A century after John Winthrop and the first Puritans arrived to establish the Massachusetts Bay Colony, most residents had become at least partly secularized. They slowly grew weary of hellfire sermons and conversions. Their attention was diverted by war and by the daily concerns of business.

In 1750 Edwards was dismissed from his pulpit at Northampton. He became pastor of a frontier church in Stockbridge, where he tried with difficulty to convert the Indians. Edwards continued to publish philosophical essays and was appointed president of the respected College of New Jersey (now Princeton University) in 1757. In January 1758, shortly after he arrived in Princeton, Edwards contracted smallpox and died.

21

1761

James Otis declares, "Taxation without representation is tyranny."

JUST AS THE FRENCH REVOLUTION WAS KNOWN FOR the rallying cry of "Liberty, equality, fraternity," so the American Revolution had its own slogan, "Taxation without representation is tyranny." These few words summed up directly the dilemma of colonists from Massachusetts to Georgia.

In 1761, King George III, then recently installed on the British throne, issued a "writ of assistance." Intended to enforce long-neglected customs laws, this writ was an open-ended warrant for British officials to search homes, warehouses, and ships for smuggled goods. Neither the goods nor the homes to be searched needed to be named on the writ of assistance for it to be enforceable.

In February 1761, several Boston merchants chose to challenge the writ of assistance in court. They hired thirty-six-year-old lawyer James Otis, whose father—also named James Otis—was the politically powerful Speaker of the Massachusetts House of Representatives. Highly regarded for legal erudition and for an easily provoked temper, the younger Otis refused to accept any fee for the privilege of challenging royal power in the person of Thomas Hutchinson, the commonwealth's chief justice. A notable Tory sympathizer without any legal experience, Hutchinson had received his appointment to the bench over Otis's father.

In his court argument, Otis applied several basic principles of common law and natural law. Citizens have a right to protection against forced entry as long as they behave peacefully in their own homes—in other words, a man's home is his castle. Otis further reminded the court that arbitrary acts by King Charles I had cost Charles his throne and his head.

In an address lasting four hours, Otis enunciated many a tenet of natural law, those unchanging principles common to all human beings. According to notes taken by John Adams, who at the time was a young lawyer from Quincy, one of those tenets was that "taxation without representation is tyranny." Adams didn't publish his notes until 1773, and no contemporary transcript exists to verify Otis's words. Nevertheless, these became watchwords of a growing antiroyalist faction.

22

1764-65

The Sugar Act and the Stamp Act arouse antiroyalist sentiments.

THE FRENCH AND INDIAN WAR WAS FOUGHT FROM 1754 to 1763. British forces and their colonial allies in America ultimately proved victorious over the French, who had received assistance from Native American tribes. In 1760, several hundred Massachusetts soldiers were notably part of a British force that successfully attacked the French outpost in Quebec. The Treaty of Paris in 1763 consolidated this and other British victories. All French territories in North America, except New Orleans, were then ceded to England.

Rather than reinforcing British rule in the colonies, the British triumph in the French and Indian War served to undermine it. The thirteen English colonies, led by men such as Benjamin Franklin, began to see a need to unite for their common defense. In addition, George Washington and other American military leaders had received considerable battle experience; they would put such lessons to use later against their former allies.

When the war finally ended, profit-minded Boston merchants were ready to resume the commerce that hostilities had interrupted. The British, likewise, saw an opportunity to replenish a treasury drained by years of conflict. In 1764 King George III signed the first of a series of tax acts that severely provoked his colonial subjects. The Sugar Act decreed a tax on refined sugar and molasses purchased from non-British sources in the French and Dutch West Indies.

In 1765 the Stamp Act sought to raise additional revenue for the British from a tax—verified by an affixed stamp—to be imposed on all colonial newspapers, legal papers, and other printed matter. In Boston and elsewhere, anti-British agitators calling themselves the "Sons of Liberty" began to practice an early form of civil disobedience. The Bostonians refused to purchase or sell any tax stamps, as British law required. They also organized a boycott of all imported British goods. A "Stamp Act Congress" comprising outraged representatives from nine American colonies, including Massachusetts, met in New York in October 1765.

Parliament reluctantly repealed the Stamp Act in March 1766, though the legislators insisted on reaffirming London's right to tax the colonies. The point was obviously crucial if Great Britain were to maintain effective control of its overseas territories. A year later, a stubborn Parliament passed the Townshend Acts, which levied taxes on paper, paint, tea, and other goods imported to the colonies. Again Bostonians organized a boycott.

The Sons of Liberty, with Samuel Adams as their leader, controlled an increasingly rebellious Massachusetts legislature. The General Court sent a "Circular Letter" to other colonial assemblies, inviting them to join in the Massachusetts boycott of British goods and ships. All agreed. In turn, the Crown ordered customs agents sent to Boston to enforce its will. By the end of 1768, two regiments of the British army were stationed in Boston. In the end, the arrival of troops only stiffened the resistance of patriots who feared more than anything the repressive presence of a "standing army."

23

1765

John Singleton Copley submits a portrait for exhibition at the Royal Academy in London.

THE UNSIGNED SUBMISSION TO THE SOCIETY OF Artists in London—a portrait in oils titled *Boy with a Squirrel*—carried an unmistakable clue to its exotic origin: the tiny animal depicted in the painting was a species native to the eastern American forests. And yet the painter's style was masterful, which puzzled the judges: surely no untutored American could possibly have used a brush with such sublime grace.

Among those who viewed the mysterious painting was Sir Joshua Reynolds, London's greatest portrait painter. Reynolds hailed the artist as "a genius" and advised that the unnamed person come to Europe and study the masters. Benjamin West, a Philadelphia-born Londoner who was a founder-member of the Royal Academy of Arts, raved, too. "What delicious coloring," he gushed, "worthy of Titian himself." Yet the rules of the Society of Artists forbade the exhibition of any anonymous work. At last, the artist was revealed as John Singleton Copley, twenty-seven, of Boston.

He may have been unknown to London, but in Boston Copley was already a successful portraitist whose work had made him wealthy. Elegant renderings of ladies wearing elbow-high satin gloves and gentlemen snugly buttoned in their waistcoats earned him a following among the city's elite and a constant stream of commissions. He also painted memorable portraits of notable political figures, such as Samuel Adams, John Hancock, and Paul Revere (in which the silversmith pensively regards a silver bowl of his own making).

John Singleton Copley was born in Boston in 1738 of parents who recently had immigrated from Ireland. Richard Copley, his father, owned a tobacco shop on Long Wharf, but he died when his son was not yet ten years old. Fatefully for the boy, Mary Copley soon married Peter Pelham, an engraver, portrait painter, and schoolmaster. Pelham taught his trade to his precocious stepson. Copley accepted his first portrait commissions when he was only fifteen.

According to those subjects who patiently sat for him, Copley was a painstaking painter. For a portrait, he required from fifteen to as many as twenty-five sittings, each of six hours' duration. He spent most of that time simply looking at his subject, and he was said to have the sharpest eye of any painter in the colonies. Unlike many portraitists of the time, Copley made only a few preparatory drawings. When he was ready, he painted directly on the blank canvas, mixing his own colors as he worked.

Copley submitted *Boy with a Squirrel* anonymously as a matter of pride. He wanted his peers in London to judge his work by European standards, which presumably were far higher than their standards for a work produced in the colonies. The warm critical reception for the portrait came as a personal vindication and an enticement to move his studio to the home country. At the same time, the businessman in Copley realized he would have much more competition for work in London than in Boston, and he wondered whether he could prosper, or even survive, there.

Copley, who was loyal to the British crown, remained in Boston and watched in confusion as the city was engulfed in political turmoil. One of his former portrait subjects, Samuel Adams, led the infamous Boston Tea Party. The tea dumped into Boston Harbor was consigned to Copley's father-in-law, an ominous harbinger of coming violence against Royalists. In 1774 John Singleton Copley—the first American painter taken seriously by European artists and critics—left his native city for London and never returned.

24 | 1770

British troops stationed in Boston fire on a mob, killing five men.

A FAMOUS ENGRAVING BY PAUL REVERE SHOWS a neat line of British Redcoats firing into a horrified crowd of colonists. Titled "The Bloody Massacre Perpetrated in King Street," it purports to portray the events of March 5, 1770. In reality, it's a piece of propaganda that doesn't really reflect what happened in what's now known as the Boston Massacre.

Indeed, very little about Revere's work stands up to what is known of the events of March 5, 1770. That late winter's evening in Boston, dozens of young men gathered to taunt a lone British sentry. Snow and ice were packed on the ground along King Street (now State Street), convenient ingredients for snowballs and iceballs. Tensions in the city had slowly been building since the "damned rascally scoundrel lobsters" had arrived nearly eighteen months earlier.

In short order, anxious British soldiers left a nearby barracks to aid their solitary comrade. As word spread, church bells pealed an alarm, and angry townspeople poured through surrounding streets and alleys. A patriot named Crispus Attucks left a waterfront tavern and rounded up a group of men who wielded clubs and other weapons. Six feet tall and powerfully built, Attucks (also known as Michael Johnson) was a person of color, though historians today are uncertain whether he was a former slave, a full-blooded member of the Natick tribe, or someone of mixed blood.

Seven British grenadiers, armed with bayoneted muskets, valiantly fought the urge to defend themselves against the mob that faced them. Standing not far from the Old State House, Capt. Thomas Preston instructed his men to load their rifles, though he withheld the order to fire.

The besieged men could no longer withstand snowballs, stones, and taunts. At last they began firing into the crowd. Before the first shots rang

Site of the Boston Massacre

out, the Bostonians believed the British had loaded their weapons only with powder. But now several of their fellow citizens had fallen to the ground wounded, dead, or dying. Eleven men were eventually hit by the soldiers' bullets; three were killed instantly and another two lay mortally wounded. Among the dead was Attucks, the first person of color to fall in the American cause of freedom.

In the immediate aftermath of the Boston Massacre, two Adams men figured prominently. Samuel Adams, firebrand and leader of the Sons of Liberty, organized a rally the following day at Faneuil Hall to demand that British soldiers withdraw from Boston. Later, his cousin John Adams agreed to defend Capt. Preston and his soldiers, who were charged with murder. John Adams was also a member of the Sons of Liberty, but despite his political sentiments he refused to see men sent to the gallows unjustly.

For his defense, John Adams relied on the testimony of several witnesses who rebutted the allegation that Preston had ordered his men to fire. The young lawyer also painted the Boston mob as provocateurs. After two and a half hours of deliberation, the jury in the Boston Massacre trial returned with its verdict: Capt. Preston and five of his men were not guilty. Two others in the dock, however, were convicted of manslaughter, and as punishment the men were branded on their thumbs.

25 1773

Phillis Wheatley publishes the first book by an African American poet.

IN 1761, A YOUNG AFRICAN GIRL ARRIVED IN BOSTON aboard the slave ship *Phillis* and was sold to Mrs. Susannah Wheatley. Her new owner noticed that the girl was losing her front baby teeth and concluded that she was about eight years old. She named her Phillis for the ship that had transported her.

Over the next six years, while Phillis Wheatley worked as a domestic servant, she was tutored by Mary Wheatley, Susannah's teenage daughter. Phillis quickly learned to speak English and later learned Latin. She also mastered the Bible and classical mythology.

The Wheatley family apparently treated their slave like an adopted daughter, and she was a frequent guest in the homes of many wealthy Bostonians. The Wheatleys also warmly encouraged the girl's gift for poetic self-expression, and Phillis's first published poem appeared in the *Newport Mercury* on December 21, 1767, when she was merely thirteen years old. Her poem on the death of evangelist minister George Whitefield, published three years later, helped gain considerable fame for its author.

When a notice appeared in the *Boston Censor* on February 29, 1772, asking for subscribers to "A Collection of POEMS, wrote at several times, and upon various occasions, by PHILLIS, a Negro Girl," well-read Bostonians would have discerned the author's identity quickly. Nevertheless, despite several notices, not enough people pledged to purchase the book. A determined Susannah Wheatley next pursued printers in London. When one was found willing, he was skeptical enough to demand proof that the author truly was what the manuscript represented—an African-born slave.

Eventually, the Massachusetts governor, lieutenant governor, and more than a dozen other prominent citizens of the commonwealth, including John Hancock, signed a statement attesting that the poet was "a young

Negro Girl, who was but a few Years since, brought an uncultivated Barbarian from Africa, and has ever since been, and now is, under the Disadvantage of serving as a Slave in a Family in this Town." The printer was satisfied, and the author's notoriety was ensured.

In 1773 Wheatley traveled to London and was received as a celebrity by the Earl of Dartmouth and other nobility. Her book *Poems on Various Subjects, Religious and Moral* was later published in Boston.

In March 1776, days before the British Army evacuated Boston, George Washington invited Wheatley to his Cambridge headquarters. A refugee of war now living in Providence, the poet had composed a poem in the general's honor. Ironically, the freed Boston slave and the Virginia slave owner discussed the subject of American liberty.

26

1773

Bostonians protest a tax on tea by throwing a shipment into Boston Harbor.

AFTER SEVERAL ATTEMPTS TO IMPOSE TAXES ON the colonists, most of which were unsuccessful, the British Parliament approved the Tea Act in April 1773. This new legislation was primarily meant to shore up the all-but-bankrupt East India Company, which held a powerful royal monopoly on trade in spices, silk, and tea.

The bill provided the giant mercantile firm, which owed the British government £1 million in back taxes, with a £1.5 million loan written on generous terms. Parliament also allowed the company a virtual monopoly on the tea trade in the colonies. Lastly, it reaffirmed an existing three-pence tax on East India's tea.

Boston merchants received word of the Tea Act with anger not only because it revived the prickly issue of Parliament's right to tax the colonies but also because its monopolistic provisions restricted a profitable trade in importing tea. John Hancock, one of the wealthiest men in the colonies, faced a considerable loss of income, and he was not alone. Urged on by Samuel Adams, the Sons of Liberty called for a boycott on East India tea. They threatened to name any violators as traitors.

On November 28, 1773, the *Dartmouth* landed in Boston Harbor at Griffin's Wharf (near today's Rowe's Wharf). The ship carried a cargo of East India Company tea as well as other commodities. Its arrival stirred the Sons of Liberty to action. Adams called a series of meetings at Faneuil Hall and organized a committee to watch the ship so that none of its tea would be unloaded.

According to customs law, the owner of a ship had twenty days to pay the necessary tax on its cargo or the cargo would be seized for nonpayment of duties. The owner of the *Dartmouth* spent three weeks attending near-riotous town meetings of patriots and heated discussions with the heavy-handed governor, Thomas Hutchinson. The harried merchant simply hoped to save his cargo and his ship, one way or another. It became clear, however, that the patriots would not allow anything to be unloaded from the *Dartmouth*—or for it to leave the port.

On December 16, with the twenty days' grace period nearly expired, Sam Adams gave a signal, and a crowd at Old South Meeting House began to whoop and make other warlike cries. Throughout the day, Bostonians had fanned the flames of their emotions with flagons of ale at the Green Dragon tavern. Patriots poured into the streets and headed for the wharf where the *Dartmouth* was tied beside two other tea ships, the *Beaver* and the *Eleanor*.

Many in the crowd who approached Griffin's Wharf that night were dressed as Mohawk Indians. They wore blankets wrapped around their shoulders and feathers in their hair; their white faces were darkened with charcoal. When they got aboard the *Dartmouth*, they began to work methodically. In three hours they dumped tons of tea overboard but touched nothing else. Before they left for shore, the "Mohawks" swept the ships' decks clean and submitted to inspections to guard against unsanctioned smuggling.

Tea from what became known as the Boston Tea Party so thoroughly polluted Boston Harbor that it clogged shipping lanes. As punishment, Parliament quickly passed legislation that closed the city's port to all but ships delivering food and fuel.

27

Paul Revere and other riders warn colonists that British regulars are marching on Concord.

THE PAUL REVERE PORTRAYED IN HENRY Wadsworth Longfellow's famous poem bears little resemblance to the Paul Revere who rode toward Lexington on the night of April 18, 1775. Revere did not even finish the famous ride—nor did he ride alone to every Middlesex village and farm: William Dawes, Dr. Samuel Prescott, and perhaps as many as sixty other riders were involved.

Nevertheless, Paul Revere remains today an exemplary figure of early American history, a man of great artistic skill who combined personal courage with public audacity. Before he hopped astride "Brown Beauty" in Charlestown, Revere already stood in the first rank of Boston patriots.

A silversmith and metallurgist by trade, Paul Revere published an engraving of the Boston Massacre (see page 41) that proved pivotal to the patriots' cause. in galvanizing public opinion against the British. In 1773 he was one of the patriots dumping tea off the *Dartmouth* into Boston Harbor. He served, too, as a principal rider for Boston's Committee of Safety—a revolutionary citizens' group that later helped organize the Minutemen— and had traveled to New York and Philadelphia.

On Saturday, April 15, 1775, Revere and others in Boston noticed an alarming trend in British troop movements. Routine patrols were canceled, and work began to ready troop boats for action. The patriots surmised that the British were preparing either to arrest John Hancock and Sam Adams, who were in Lexington for a meeting of the Massachusetts Provincial Congress, or else to seize a cache of arms hidden in nearby Concord. Early on the following morning, April 16, Revere rode to Lexington to warn Adams and Hancock. The militia in Concord was similarly advised of possible trouble.

On his way back to Boston later that day, Revere and the Charlestown Committee of Safety established the famous signal to be hung in the North Church tower: one lantern if the British were leaving Boston by land (via Boston Neck), two if by water (across the Charles River).

On the night of April 18, British troop action reached a fever pitch. Revere was rowed by friends across the mouth of the Charles River to Charlestown, where he received a horse and galloped off.

According to depositions given years later, Revere reached Lexington at midnight, and William Dawes arrived a half hour later. They rode together to Concord, where Samuel Prescott joined them. Somewhere on the road, British troops halted and tried to arrest the trio. Prescott galloped off and escaped; Dawes rode back in the direction of Lexington and likewise eluded capture; Revere, on the other hand, looked down at raised pistols and wisely yielded.

The British soldiers and their prisoners returned to Lexington, where Revere was immediately released. He went once again to where Adams and Hancock were staying and was able to see them off before British troops arrived at Lexington Green for a fateful confrontation with the Minutemen.

28

1775

The Revolutionary War begins in Lexington and Concord.

THE MINUTEMEN OF LEXINGTON ASSEMBLED haphazardly on the town green in the early morning of April 19, 1775, not quite sure what they should do. They knew only of Paul Revere's warning that Redcoats were approaching the town in military formation. Several of those under Capt. John Parker's command had not even bothered to bring ammunition for their muskets.

North Bridge, Concord

Acting with royal authority, British Major John Pitcairn called on the Americans to lay down their arms and disperse. The Minutemen replied by falling out of ranks, but they resolutely held onto their weapons. British officers repeated the call to disarm, without success. A shot was fired, though from which side will never be clear. The American Revolutionary War had begun.

The well-trained British let fly with one volley, then another. Eight Massachusetts men soon lay dead on Lexington Green; ten writhed in pain from their wounds. Struck by a British ball, Capt. Parker was finished off with a redcoat bayonet thrust. The Minutemen had returned the fire unconvincingly: one British soldier received only a flesh wound in his leg.

Quickly, Major Pitcairn led his men away to Concord, where they hoped to seize a hidden store of weapons. The British, who were swaggering now, marched to the music of fife and drum. Traveling in the opposite direction were Sam Adams and John Hancock, who had earlier received Revere's warning to flee. Adams remarked about the glorious morning, and Hancock apparently thought his carriage companion referred to the weather. "I mean," said Adams, "what a glorious morning for America."

At Concord's North Bridge, the British crossed the Concord River to take the house of Col. James Barrett, where they had heard that the Minutemen's arms were stockpiled. When the British set fires in the town courthouse and elsewhere, Concord's defenders—who were outnumbered and, up to this point, had held their fire—now descended on British companies at the North Bridge. The element of surprise was in the Massachusetts men's favor, and the Redcoats took their first serious casualties, including three dead. (Two British soldiers remain buried at the North Bridge.)

In short order, the British began a disorderly afternoon retreat back to Boston under intermittent fire from local militia. After nearly forty miles of marching, the Redcoats ended where they began, though they arrived in Charlestown not half as confident as when they had departed. From there to Concord lay a bloody chain of dead and wounded Redcoats side by side with American civilian casualties. Approximately fifty Massachusetts men and seventy-five British soldiers were killed. Several hundred altogether were wounded on both sides, with the British bearing the greater losses.

From headquarters hastily set up at Cambridge, Dr. Joseph Warren, a leading Boston physician and head of the local Committee of Safety, heard news of the battle and sounded a general call to arms. Soon twenty thousand volunteers were milling about in Harvard Yard. The men were prepared to enlist in the army of a nation that as yet had no name.

29

1775

Dr. Joseph Warren dies in the Battle of Bunker Hill.

FROM OPPOSITE SIDES OF THE CHARLES RIVER basin in 1775, the peninsulas of Boston and Charlestown were like the pincers of a lobster poised to snap shut. Three hills in Charlestown—Breed's, Bunker's (now known simply as Bunker Hill), and Moulton's—afforded fine views of the North End and other parts of the nearby town center. Likewise, Dorchester Heights—a hammer-shaped peninsula south of Boston—commanded a clear view of Boston's flank as well as of the harbor's entrance.

In June, Gen. Thomas Gage, commanding the British forces in Boston, and Gen. Artemus Ward, commanding the newborn American army based in Cambridge, looked with equal longing on these positions. Any army wishing either to hold or to surround Boston would find the Charlestown hills and Dorchester desirable outposts.

Responding to a call from the Committee of Safety, General Ward sent a detachment under Col. William Prescott to a nearly deserted Charlestown on the night of June 16. Ordered to fortify Bunker's Hill, Prescott and his American troops instead began to dig their defenses at Breed's Hill. The choice was probably not accidental, for while Breed's Hill was shorter than Bunker, it was closer to Boston.

At dawn, British ships in the harbor began shelling the still-unfinished American position, but with little effect. Far worse damage was to come in the early afternoon, when a force of fifteen hundred British under Gen. William Howe landed in longboats at the Charlestown waterfront for an attack on Breed's Hill. An incendiary shell fell to earth, and Charlestown began to burn.

On Breed's Hill, the American forces included Dr. Joseph Warren, recently commissioned a major general. The Yankees held their fire until the advancing Redcoats came within fifty yards of their positions. The delaying tactic was prompted by a need to conserve ammunition, but it has since given rise to the legend that Col. Prescott ordered his men, "Don't fire till you see the whites of their eyes." In fact, the remark was something of a military cliché; it was probably first made at least thirty years earlier, by Frederick the Great of Prussia.

Withering musket fire ripped through the British lines as they made their first charge up Breed's Hill. A second assault met the same fierce welcome. The Redcoats turned their muskets and their bayonets on anyone still inside the stronghold. When their ammunition was gone, the Americans retreated, with British fusiliers hot on their heels.

June 17 took a bloody toll on both sides. British officers who accompanied Gen. Howe to Breed's Hill lay dead or wounded. In addition, 226 British infantry were dead, 828 wounded. For the Americans, 140 had died, 271 were wounded. Dr. Warren was among the last to flee; he died from a bullet in the back that killed him instantly. He was buried in an unmarked grave later that day on Breed's Hill, and Gen. Howe remarked that his opponent's death was worth five hundred men to him.

While the Redcoats "won" the Battle of Bunker Hill, their losses were shockingly heavy. General Nathanael Greene famously said, after the battle, "I wish we could sell them another hill at the same price." Patriot resolve was stiffened in the wake of the battle, and never again did the Redcoats attack an American position with such brash confidence.

30

1775

The Hannah receives its wartime commission from Gen. George Washington.

THE FIRST SETTLERS OF ROCKY MARBLEHEAD WERE probably regarded by their pious Puritan neighbors in Salem as destined to writhe for eternity in the fires of hell. Descendants of Cornish fishermen, the early Marbleheaders were likewise disdainful of their faithful fellow citizens. They had come to America for the good fishing, after all, not for the church services. And the fishing in waters off Marblehead made for very good eating indeed—which was more than could be said for most ministers' sermons.

When British forces closed the port of Boston in 1774 as punishment for the city's revolutionary behavior, Marbleheaders eagerly seized a business opportunity. The town's port was opened to all vessels previously destined for Boston's wharves. Marblehead also became a refuge for privateers who went to sea in search of profit and a bit of old-fashioned hell-raising. Local Tory merchants and British merchant marine captains were terrorized equally.

In 1775, Gen. George Washington, in command of the Continental Army at Cambridge, gave orders for the military conversion of the *Hannah*, a fifty-two-foot, seventy-eight-ton Grand Banks schooner. Although the *Hannah* was registered in Marblehead and had a Marblehead crew, its owner, John Glover, chose to launch the retrofitted vessel from a Beverly wharf. As a result, both towns claim to be the birthplace of the American

Navy. When the *Hannah* received its wartime commission in August, Marblehead skipper Nicholson Broughton was commander.

The *Hannah* was not intended to take on British naval vessels but to strike at cargo ships carrying vital foodstuffs, arms, and other goods. Rather than take on the British merchant marine, which might have risked the wrath of His Majesty's navy, Capt. Broughton preferred to commandeer American vessels. When he returned to port, he easily could claim that the confiscated goods were those of the enemy.

With another Marblehead fishing captain, John Selman, Broughton also sailed the *Hannah* to Nova Scotia, where the pair of privateers razed a village and kidnapped several people. When Capt. Broughton returned with his loot and prisoners to Gen. Washington in Cambridge, he was disappointed to find his commanding officer embarrassed rather than pleased. On Washington's orders, Broughton's prisoners were released, and the Marbleheader's navy commission expired without renewal.

On Christmas Day 1776, Gen. Glover's "amphibious regiment" cunningly used muffled oars to row Gen. Washington and his men across the Delaware River for a sneak attack against British and Hessian troops in Trenton, New Jersey.

31

1776

British Redcoats evacuate Boston.

IN JULY 1775, ONLY A FEW WEEKS AFTER THE Battle of Bunker Hill, Gen. George Washington arrived in Cambridge to take command of the Continental Army. He studied intently the bloody lessons of June 17 but was not ready to show off his conclusions for eight months.

From the start, Washington faced severe obstacles in his ambition to drive the British army from Boston. The men under his command were not like any soldiers he had ever led before. The Virginian patrician was appalled to find, for example, that Massachusetts militiamen elected their own officers.

In addition, Washington lacked the heavy guns necessary to threaten General Howe and his Redcoats convincingly. Ethan Allen and the Green Mountain Boys of Vermont had captured the British cannons at Ticonderoga, New York, in May 1775. If those powerful guns—more than fifty of them—could be brought to Boston, Washington would have his arsenal.

Accordingly, Gen. Henry Knox of Boston, formerly a bookseller, was dispatched to Ticonderoga to handle the formidable task. He chose to wait for winter when muddy roads would harden and then transported the heavy artillery on sleds hauled by teams of oxen. In three months, Knox—a large man who resembled something of an ox himself—had successfully completed the journey of more than two hundred miles.

While he waited for Knox, Washington felt the sting of public criticism for his inaction. At last, in February 1776, he was prepared to strike at his enemy across the Charles River. Washington's study of the Battle of Bunker Hill told him that Col. Prescott might have fared better if his partially constructed fortifications hadn't failed to hold back the full brunt of the British attack. With the help of Col. Rufus Putnam, Washington ordered a kind of ready-made fort to be prepared for transportation to Dorchester Heights, just south of Boston, in easy-to-assemble sections.

On the morning of March 5, General Howe saw an amazing sight that had not been there the night before: a line of well-made fortifications—replete with the cannons from Ticonderoga—on Dorchester Heights. Rear Adm. Molyneaux Shuldham, commanding the Royal Navy in Boston Harbor, warned Howe that his ships could not remain long as sitting targets of any heavy guns placed on the heights. A frustrated Howe chose to abandon his positions at Boston.

On March 17, 1776, the last British ship loaded with men and supplies soon pulled away from Boston's docks to positions elsewhere in the colonies. A tacit agreement was reached with the American forces to allow the Redcoats to evacuate the town without disruption as long as they would not burn it.

Across the colonies, George Washington was hailed for achieving a blood-
less victory that freed forever the seat of the American rebellion. Among
other honors, the Virginian received an honorary doctorate of laws from
Harvard College.

32

John Adams drafts the Massachusetts Constitution.

"ALL MEN ARE BORN FREE AND EQUAL," DECLARES
the first article of the Constitution of the Commonwealth of Massachusetts. That simple statement has
proven immensely powerful. With seven words, its
author, John Adams, shifted forever the balance of
political power from a few who ruled by divine right to the many who
ruled themselves by human right.

In a true revolution, nothing remains of the past. The American
Revolution—in which a group of colonies for the first time had removed
themselves from the power of a distant monarch—theoretically left the
new country without laws or government. Perhaps not surprisingly, men
such as John Adams, Benjamin Franklin, Thomas Jefferson, and others
involved in shaping the new country's government showed reverence
toward the past. They greatly admired the Roman republic and also
Athenian democracy.

These men of British descent also cherished the mother country's unwritten constitution and its common law. As the Declaration of Independence
makes clear, any argument with England was not with its people or its
traditions but with the king. ("He has refused his Assent to Laws. . . . He
has obstructed the Administration of Justice. . . . He has plundered our
Seas. . . .")

Those appointed with the responsibility to make laws for the new country
realized that if the British system had any flaw, it was that the constitution

was unwritten. By setting out on paper the limits of a government's power, they would address this problem in the new country.

Massachusetts became the first colony to try to create a suitable written constitution. In 1778 the legislature made an attempt, but voters failed to approve this first constitution by a substantial five-to-one margin—not so much for what it said but for what it left unsaid. Newburyport's Theophilus Parsons published a pamphlet listing the most important omissions: a bill of rights, provision for separation of powers, and protection of religious freedom.

Accordingly, Massachusetts voters (for the first time, all men over twenty-one, not just those with property) chose 293 delegates to a convention with the express purpose of writing a state constitution. The Massachusetts Constitutional Convention gathered for the first time in Cambridge on September 1, 1779. Among their number were Samuel Adams, Robert Treat Paine, and James Bowdoin as well as John Adams and Theophilus Parsons. A vote by committee gave John Adams much of the editorial responsibility. He submitted a draft before he had to leave for Holland, where he was beginning his duties as ambassador. Throughout the spring of 1780, at town meetings across Massachusetts, voters examined the document clause by clause and ultimately gave their approval.

Anyone wondering how Massachusetts came to be called a commonwealth need look no further than the state's constitution, which in Adams's words was specifically a "declaration of rights and frame of government [for] the commonwealth of Massachusetts." Adams owed the term to Thomas Hobbes and John Locke, English political philosophers who described the body politic as the "commonwealth" or "commonweal" (in Old English, weal was the term for welfare or good). "Commonwealth" was also the name given to Oliver Cromwell's antiroyalist republic that ruled Great Britain from the execution of King Charles I in 1649 until the restoration of the monarchy with Charles II in 1660. In English politics, then, a "commonwealth" came to evoke the notion of a government by the people rather than an aristocracy. (Among the fifty states, Massachusetts, Kentucky, Pennsylvania, and Virginia are officially "commonwealths," though the title confers no legal distinction from the other states.)

The Massachusetts Constitution was a model document in many ways, and seven years later the framers of the U.S. Constitution modeled their document on it and on the constitutions of other states. The United States, however, would take far longer to follow the commonwealth's lead in abolishing slavery. In Massachusetts, those opening words, "All men are born free and equal," were quickly interpreted to include slaves. Several lawsuits successfully challenged the constitutionality of slavery in Massachusetts. By 1790 a census found no slaves living anywhere in the commonwealth.

33

1784

The Empress of China leaves Boston, beginning the China trade.

A PROUD DANIEL PARKER AND HIS BUSINESS partners touted their new vessel in heroic terms in a report to their insurance agents: "She was Built in Boston under the direction of the Celebrated Mr. Peck [John Peck, Boston's master shipwright] on a Model that is universally acknowledged in this Country to be greatly superior to any other. . . . She is entirely New, Stout, Staunch & Strong. Her Bottom was Coppered in Boston with great attention & Care & her Hull is as fully Strongly & Compleately finished as this country is capable of doing it." These claims might help keep down the cost of insurance premiums, but the *Empress of China* needed to prove Parker and the others right if they were going to reap any profit from their investments.

In November 1783 the *Empress of China* left its shipyard dock for New York to meet captain, crew, and cargo. When the boat finally sailed past Fort George, New York, in February 1784, it already enjoyed a reputation as "an exceeding swift sailor."

The first time out, the vessel would be well tested. Capt. John Green planned to take the 400-ton vessel and crew of 42 sailors on a southeasterly course past the Cape of Good Hope in South Africa, north through the

Indian Ocean, and finally into port at Canton, at the South China Sea. Altogether, Green anticipated a grueling 180-day, 18,000-mile voyage.

Deep in the enormous boat's hold lay a precious cargo of American ginseng root, fifteen tons in all. The supposedly medicinal plant was one of the few products from the Western world that interested Chinese merchants, for native ginseng was a scarce commodity. The Chinese believed that ginseng root soothed nerves, lengthened life, and cleared up acne. In May 1785, fifteen months after departing New York, the *Empress of China* returned laden with what Americans and Europeans treasured even more than a long life and a good complexion: silk and jade. And China was open for business.

"The China trade" was conducted from the commonwealth's busy wharves at Boston, Salem, and Newburyport. Merchants' attention slowly began to shift from Europe and the West Indies to Africa and the Far East. Massachusetts boats became frequent visitors to Cape Town, Zanzibar, and Burma. As the eighteenth century ended, Salem's captains briefly cornered the world market in black pepper. In contemporary terms, such a trading coup was as valuable as holding an international franchise on silicon chips.

34
1786

Daniel Shays leads a revolt against the state and federal governments.

MASSACHUSETTS RELIED INCREASINGLY ON MERCHANT trade for its wealth as the eighteenth century ended, but agriculture remained the bedrock of its economy. In the years just after the Revolution, "yeomen" farmers made up 70 percent of the rural population. When those farmers faced financial ruin and foreclosure in the depression that followed the signing of a peace treaty with England in 1783, everyone in the commonwealth felt the shock.

Peasant rebellions have occurred regularly throughout medieval and modern history and usually are indicators of economic hardship. When deprived farmers have seen family and friends starve or be driven off their land, insurrection becomes a means to achieve justice or, at least, a measure of revenge.

In 1785 the commonwealth's legislators toed a line drawn by Boston merchants and revoked the legal tender of Massachusetts's paper money. As a result, many debts, including those for taxes, were to be paid only in silver or gold coin. Farmers, who usually paid debts in produce and could not easily come up with the required "specie," found themselves hauled into court by creditors.

At the hands of unsympathetic judges, hundreds of farmers suffered the indignities of foreclosure and property loss. Desperate yeomen in five counties near Springfield took up arms in the summer of 1786 and marched to prevent several courthouses from opening. Among those leading the insurgents was Daniel Shays, who had served with distinction in the Revolution, fighting at Lexington and in the Battle of Bunker Hill as well as at Ticonderoga, Stony Point, and Saratoga. Many in his ranks, who were called "Shaysites," were war veterans aware that power flows from the barrel of a gun.

In January 1787 Shays approached the Springfield federal arsenal with twelve hundred men. The farmers' goal was to overthrow the Massachusetts state government, and the arsenal's cache of muskets, powder, shot, and shell made a logical target. As the rebels charged, loyal militiamen fired their cannons. Four farmers fell dead; another twenty were wounded. The survivors quickly broke ranks.

For another month, the yeoman insurgents moved like a guerrilla army. They raided the stores of hated shopkeepers and played cat-and-mouse with the state militia. After defeat in a clash with troops in Petersham, Shays escaped across the border to Vermont, which was then an independent republic. The rebellion disappeared with him. Shays was later condemned to death along with thirteen other rebel leaders, but he and the others were eventually pardoned and allowed to return to their farms. The state legislature was also moved to ease penalties for debtors who fell afoul of their creditors.

35

1795

Charles Bulfinch supervises construction of the Massachusetts State House.

WHEN JOHN WINTHROP DECLARED THAT NEW England should be "as a city upon a hill," he envisioned that Puritan Boston would serve as a moral beacon for the world. Beacon Hill was named in a more literal sense, however, for a torch left blazing at its summit that guided ships safely into Boston Harbor. For the past two centuries, the promontory's only true beacon, moral or otherwise, has been the spectacular dome of the Massachusetts State House.

At a ceremony on July 4, 1795, fifteen white horses (representing the fifteen states in the Union that year) drew a cart that carried the new State House cornerstone to the top of Beacon Hill. Massachusetts Governor Samuel Adams and his fellow patriot Paul Revere laid the stone in place as Charles Bulfinch watched. The young architect had waited eight years to see the work begin.

Bulfinch, a Boston native and son of one of the city's wealthiest families, studied at Harvard College during the Revolutionary War period and graduated in 1781. Dr. Thomas Bulfinch dissuaded his son from taking up the practice of medicine, and at least until 1789, Charles Bulfinch's occupation appears in the town directory only as "gentleman."

From 1785 to 1787, Bulfinch traveled through Europe on an inheritance. At the suggestion of Thomas Jefferson, he toured the major architectural sites of France and Italy and was especially impressed by the architecture of late Georgian London. In November 1787, not long after returning to Boston, Bulfinch, then barely twenty-four years old, boldly submitted "a plan for a new Statehouse" to a legislative committee that was charged "to consider a more convenient Place for holding the General Court." The architect's inspiration for the State House design was likely Somerset House in London, a government building designed by Sir William Chambers in

1778 in a symmetrical style Bulfinch greatly admired. Bulfinch's plan languished until the commonwealth's legislature finally gathered enough courage to approve it in February 1795. In the meantime, Bulfinch successfully designed the Connecticut State House (now Hartford City Hall) and was becoming well regarded for his elegant neoclassical work.

When he designed the Massachusetts State House, Bulfinch did not have Beacon Hill specifically in mind as the site. Boston was not even guaranteed to remain the Massachusetts state capital, certainly not if Worcester or Plymouth could persuade legislators otherwise. Before 1790, Beacon Hill was relatively unsettled. That year, Charles Bulfinch designed and erected on its summit an attractive "Memorial Column" commemorating the Revolution, and in 1791 Dr. John Joy commissioned him to design the first of many Beacon Hill homes.

The direction of the city's growth shifted enough even for the Massachusetts General Court to take notice. In 1795, Boston purchased John Hancock's pasture on the south face of Beacon Hill and designated it as the site of the new capitol building. The General Court appropriated £8,000 for the building's construction, but Bulfinch knew better. "My own experience," he warned, "has convinced me of the fallacy of estimates in general, and especially in buildings of a public nature." His concern was justified when the final bill came to more than four times the original estimate.

In January 1798 a ceremonial procession marched from the old State House up Beacon Street, with Bulfinch prominently at the front. The seat of government was officially transferred. The commonwealth had closed one chapter of its history only to open another.

Charles Bulfinch is today recognized as America's first full-time architect. From 1817 to 1830, he worked on the U.S. Capitol, as the fourth in a string of architects hired to build that building.

36

1796

John Adams is elected second president of the United States.

IN 1796 JOHN ADAMS PREPARED TO VACATE A government post he had grown to despise. The vice presidency, he wrote his wife, Abigail, was "the most insignificant office that ever the invention of man contrived or his imagination conceived." With George Washington unwilling to run for a third term, though, the nation's first vice president was chosen to serve as its second president.

Circumstances ensured that John Adams would enjoy the power of his new position even less than the inconsequence of his last. He was saddled with Thomas Jefferson as his vice president. Jefferson, a former friend turned political enemy, dogged the president's every political step. His party, the Federalists, eventually turned on Adams, too. With opponents seemingly on all sides, it is no surprise that John Adams would be the first incumbent president who failed to be reelected. In 1800 Jefferson won the election in a landslide vote; when he took office in 1801, a dour Adams retired to Massachusetts.

John Adams was a difficult to man to like. He was variously considered rude and overbearing, jealous and spiteful, vain and self-important.

The Adams family's "Old House," Quincy

Doubtless, the man had some attractive qualities; after all, few husbands are as beloved of their wives as John was of Abigail.

The peripatetic John Adams was often away from home, sometimes for years at a time (he was sent to France as a commissioner of the revolutionary government; he negotiated peace terms with the British in Ghent; and he served as America's first ambassador to the Court of St. James in London). Remaining behind with their four children, Abigail Adams managed the family farm in Braintree and maintained a fascinating correspondence with her absent mate. In 1776, when John Adams was a delegate to the Continental Congress in Philadelphia, his wife famously asked him to consider the cause of liberty from a previously neglected angle.

"Remember the ladies," Abigail Adams pleaded. "Be more generous and favorable to them than your ancestors. Do not put such unlimited power in the hands of the husbands. If particular care and attention is not paid to the ladies, we are determined to foment a rebellion, and will not hold ourselves bound by any laws in which we have no voice or representation." Women's rights were not Abigail Adams's only concern; she also expressed abhorrence of slavery and a great admiration for public education. As First Lady, she helped move the young American government to its permanent home in Washington. In 1800 the Adams family was the first to live in the still-unfinished White House.

John and Abigail's eldest son, John Quincy Adams, grew up at his father's side and traveled widely throughout Europe. President Washington appointed the young Adams ambassador to the Netherlands in 1794 when he was not yet twenty-seven years old. Later, as ambassador to Prussia, Russia, and the United Kingdom, he earned a reputation as America's greatest diplomat of that era.

In 1817 John Quincy Adams returned to America to become President James Monroe's secretary of state. Despite the name, the Monroe Doctrine of 1823 was principally Adams's work. In 1825, like his father before him, John Quincy Adams moved into the White House with lukewarm public support. Like his father, too, he was sent packing from the capital after serving a single four-year term.

In the political world of the commonwealth, however, the Adams name still carried weight. Two years after leaving Washington, John Quincy Adams returned there, not as resident of the White House, but as a member of Congress from the district of Quincy, Massachusetts. He shrugged off suggestions that the action was demeaning to the presidency and became a thorn in the side of congressional proponents of slavery.

For the next dozen years, John Quincy Adams fought gag rules preventing citizens' petitions from being heard in the House of Representatives. In 1837 he daringly presented an abolitionist petition from twenty-two slaves and was threatened with censure. In 1841 a group of Africans mutinied on the Spanish slave ship *Amistad* and brought the vessel to New York; instead of receiving the freedom they expected, the Africans were arrested and threatened with return to their owners. John Quincy Adams successfully defended their case in the U.S. Supreme Court.

As he delivered a speech against the injustices of the Mexican-American War, John Quincy Adams collapsed on the House floor and died in a congressional office two days later, February 23, 1848.

Other distinguished members of the Adams family include John Quincy's son, Charles Francis Adams, who as President Lincoln's ambassador to the United Kingdom won the important struggle to maintain that nation's neutrality in the Civil War. Charles's son, Brooks Adams, was a historian who accurately predicted that the world would one day be divided between the superpowers of Russia and the United States. Henry Adams, another son of Charles Francis Adams, admitted in his famous autobiography that as a child he expected to become president of the United States one day as a matter of birthright. For his eventual failure, Henry Adams appropriately blamed democracy.

37

1812

The "gerrymander" appears in a political cartoon condemning a redistricting plan.

OF ALL THE STRANGE POLITICAL ANIMALS TO ROAM the commonwealth, few have ever made a more enduring mark than the "gerrymander." This beast was first sighted in an 1812 editorial cartoon, when the Massachusetts state legislature—then controlled by the Democratic-Republican party—voted to rearrange the commonwealth's voting districts. To suit their political ends, Gov. Elbridge Gerry and his fellow Democratic-Republicans carved out an inelegantly shaped district of a dozen North Shore towns. In the new district, Democratic-Republican voters in Marblehead made up a majority over Federalists in Chelsea, Lynn, Danvers, Lynnfield, Andover, Methuen, Haverhill, Amesbury, and Salisbury.

It took little enough imagination to realize that the contorted new district was a bald attempt by Democratic-Republicans to shape the next election's outcome. It was left to Elkanah Tisdale, an engraver, however, to see in the curious arrangement of towns on a map a creature resembling a salamander. Tisdale drew this beast, "the Gerry-Mander," and gave it clawed feet, wings, and fangs. He published his drawing as a political cartoon in the *Boston Weekly Messenger* and added a term to the American political lexicon.

To "gerrymander" is to manipulate the boundaries of a district to give undue influence to some party or class. As a political maneuver, gerrymandering works. In 1812, only eleven Federalist state senators were elected in the commonwealth against twenty-nine Democratic-Republicans, even though the Federalists outpolled the other party statewide. The infamy of his association with the gerrymander, however, forced Governor Gerry from the state house. He was not idle for long; later that same year, former governor Gerry, who was a signer of the Declaration of Independence for Massachusetts, was elected vice president as James Madison's running mate on the winning Democratic-Republican ticket.

38

1812

The U.S. frigate Constitution earns its nickname "Old Ironsides."

IN OCTOBER 1797, THE YOUNG AMERICAN NAVY'S newest frigate, *Constitution*, was ready for launching at the Hartt Brothers Shipyard in Boston. The great vessel was the largest American warship yet built and was designed to carry 44 massive guns, though it typically had more than 50. At 204 feet long and with a displacement of 2,200 tons, *Constitution* was longer and heavier than any other ship of its kind. Paul Revere cast the bolts fastening its timbers as well as the copper sheathing for the boat's bottom.

The freshly painted *Constitution* descended the long launching cradle leading into the harbor on greased wooden planks that smoked from the tremendous friction. Suddenly the ship squealed to a stop only halfway to the water. Three more tries were required before the vessel was safely afloat.

According to sailing superstition, a launching mishap portended bad luck for the vessel. Nevertheless, *Constitution* gallantly survived several wars and narrowly escaped more menacing threats of dismantling. Today it is the oldest commissioned warship in the world.

USS Constitution

The beginning of the nineteenth century saw American merchant ships become the hapless prey of pirates, particularly from the Barbary States on the northern coast of Africa. Bandits from Tripoli regularly seized American ships and held the crews for ransom. In 1802 Congress finally declared a state of war with the Tripolitans and ordered their ports blockaded.

A still young *Constitution*, as yet untried in battle, arrived at Gibraltar in September 1803. There the frigate joined a growing fleet of navy warships patrolling in the Mediterranean. With Commodore Edward Preble commanding, *Constitution* proceeded to blockade Tripoli. Its cannons sent several punishing bombardments into the city and helped to wear down Barbar resistance. In June 1805 officials signed a treaty of peace on the decks of *Constitution*.

When Congress again declared war, in 1812, this time against the British, *Constitution* was to gain immortal fame in a contest with *Guerriere*, a Royal Navy frigate.

On August 19, *Guerriere* was eager for a duel and approached *Constitution* at pistol-firing range. An American sailor watched a British cannonball bounce off *Constitution* and exclaimed, "Good God, her sides are made of iron!" Then *Constitution* let loose with a ruthless broadside. The British navyman continued to wrestle with the American ship but never fully recovered. In an hour's time *Guerriere* surrendered.

The reputation of "Old Ironsides" grew with each passing victory. In three major engagements during the War of 1812, *Constitution* captured four British ships. The British finally agreed to end hostilities in 1815.

Thirty-one-year-old *Constitution* faced possible scrapping in 1828. A survey by the Department of the Navy had compared costs for extensive repairs necessary on the frigate with those for construction of an entirely new ship and found *Constitution* an expensive floating monument. The report was leaked to the press, and an outcry ensued.

In a poem first published in the *Boston Advertiser*, Oliver Wendell Holmes summed up public sentiment. "The meteor of the ocean air / Shall sweep the clouds no more," despaired the poet. "The harpies of the shore shall pluck / The eagle of the sea!" The Navy relented and *Constitution* continued its useful life, first on diplomatic duty and later as a training ship.

In 1927, following a public fundraising campaign that was abetted by a Hollywood feature, *Old Ironsides*, starring Wallace Beery, the great old frigate was entirely restored. Now more than two hundred years old, *Constitution* floats in a permanent berth at Charlestown.

39

1814

The American Industrial Revolution begins with steam-powered looms in Waltham.

IN 1813, WALTHAM, NINE MILES WEST OF BOSTON, was still an obscure village on the banks of the Charles River. What transformed Waltham in just a few short years would eventually transform the United States and the world: the technology of the power loom, which made possible the Industrial Revolution.

It may be said that Francis Cabot Lowell carried the battle plans for the American campaign of the Industrial Revolution in his head. In 1810 the prosperous Massachusetts merchant traveled to Great Britain with his family. He toured Manchester, a river city whose mills hummed with the activity of workers who produced vast quantities of quality textiles for markets around the world and generated sumptuous profits for the mill owners. His hosts little suspected that Lowell was too interested an observer by half.

When Lowell returned home after two years, the sharp-eyed Yankee had memorized the intricate workings of Manchester's great power looms. He and a group of investors, including his brother-in-law Patrick Jackson and Nathan Appleton, formed the Boston Manufacturing Company. English law forbade the export of manufacturing equipment or the emigration of anyone trained to operate it. To build a mill complex in Waltham, the Boston Manufacturing Company hired Paul Moody, a local mechanic who could construct what Lowell had seen and could describe.

In 1814, the country's first power loom became operational under the single roof of a fully integrated mill. The "Waltham-Lowell" system proved wildly successful. A second mill opened in 1819. A bleachery and an iron foundry, a research laboratory, and even a crayon factory soon followed.

Almost as quickly as Waltham grew, however, the limitations of the Charles River as a power source became apparent. The officers of the Boston Manufacturing Company looked elsewhere for an appropriate development site for more mills. They settled on East Chelmsford, where the Merrimack and Concord rivers met at Pawtucket Falls.

In 1796, Newburyport merchants interested in shipping timber downriver for their shipbuilding enterprises had underwritten construction of the Middlesex Canal at East Chelmsford. The canal's system of locks and aqueducts led twenty-seven miles to the Mystic River; along it, horse-drawn barges hauled goods to market. A sawmill, glassworks, and woolen mill were opened at East Chelmsford to take advantage of the convenience the new waterway afforded their businesses. In 1821 the Boston Manufacturing Company purchased the Middlesex Canal and surrounding farmland between the canal and the river. A factory town, each of its elements precisely planned and laid out, quickly rose up.

Mills, canals, stores, and housing were built as were an Episcopal church and a company cemetery. The workday began at five in the morning and ended fourteen hours later. Men received up to $8 a week for their labor. Women, newly entered into the workforce, were paid half the men's wages.

On March 1, 1826, East Chelmsford was renamed Lowell in honor of the Boston Manufacturing Company's founder. The Waltham Watch Company, manufacturer of the first machine-made watches in the United States, opened in 1854, and by century's end, Waltham was known as "Watch City." The Boston Manufacturing Company went into receivership in 1929 at the start of the Great Depression. Today the number 1 mill (built in 1813) is the site of the Charles River Museum of Industry.

40

Capt. Henry Hall of Cape Cod begins commercial cranberry cultivation.

IN SUMMER AND FALL, RIPENING WILD CRANBERRIES can transform an ordinary bog into a blazing red sea. The spreading vermilion stain gives the landscape a haunting, unearthly quality. For all its natural beauty, however, the cranberry was mostly ignored throughout the first two centuries of European settlement in Massachusetts. Not until a ship's captain in North Dennis noticed a peculiar effect of shifting sand on the cranberry plant did the commonwealth's farmers show any serious interest in the sour little fruit. Today Cape Cod cooperatives produce half of the world's crop on 12,500 acres of cranberry beds.

Only three commonly eaten fruits are native to North America: the blueberry, the Concord grape, and the cranberry. To grow properly, cranberries require an acid, peat soil; an adequate supply of fresh water; sand; and a growing season that lasts from April to November. All those conditions occur naturally on large stretches of Cape Cod, where receding glacial ice created impermeable, clay-lined "kettle hole" bogs.

According to Native American mythology, a dove carried the first cranberry from heaven to earth in its beak. (The legend later inspired the now well-recognized trademark of the Ocean Spray cranberry growers' cooperative.) In 1647, Indians at John Eliot's praying villages (see page 26) harvested wild cranberries and sold them to settlers. Throughout the eighteenth century, these wild cranberries were harvested by hand in Massachusetts and shipped to England and elsewhere in Europe, where they competed with those imported from Russia.

When the Crimean War started in 1853, the flow of the Russian crop halted, and American cranberry growers prospered by default, especially in the English market. By then, the commonwealth's farmers were ready to meet the sharply increasing demand.

Cranberry bog

The man Massachusetts cranberry growers had to thank was Henry Hall, a native of North Dennis. Born in 1760 and directly descended from an English settler who arrived on Cape Cod in 1630, Henry Hall served briefly and with no great distinction in the Revolutionary War. Town records from 1778 list "Captain" Henry Hall as owner of a sixty-nine-foot schooner, the *Viana*, which he skippered regularly between the Cape and Boston.

In 1800 Capt. Hall and two partners opened a saltworks on public land near a pond where wild cranberries had long been harvested. This swampy area, Hall observed, was submerged in winter and dry in summer. The keen-eyed captain also noticed that when sand blew over the cranberry vines, the plants were not killed but grew even more vigorously.

Ignoring ridicule from his neighbors, in 1816 Hall began to test his theories by transplanting and maintaining cranberry vines in protected fields, which he flooded in winter and then covered over with sand. Soon Hall was clearing and draining more land to create what he called "cranberry yards."

The clever Yankee had stumbled on the keys to the natural success of cranberry vine growth. According to agricultural scientists, freezing water protects delicate plants from winter damage caused by wind and snow even as a layer of windblown sand slowly collects over the thin crust. As the ice thaws in spring, the settling sand controls insect populations and stimulates the vines to put down roots. By 1820 Hall was successful enough with his cultivated cranberries to ship thirty barrels to New York for sale at produce markets. His annual yield eventually rose to unheard-of heights— seventy to a hundred bushels per acre.

Cranberries may have a naturally sour taste, but they treat farmers quite sweetly. Vines require relatively little care once they are planted, and they will spread quickly to cover available ground. Cranberry plants are virtually indestructible: Some vines on Cape Cod are more than 150 years old.

Capt. Hall's discovery may have inadvertently helped preserve tens of thousands of acres of Cape Cod wetlands. In the early nineteenth century, government officials were pushing landowners to convert marshes, bogs, and meadows into productive farmland. Cranberry cultivation, however, cannot be sustained without an extensive wetlands system and healthy aquifers. As a result, "useless" bogs were not drained to become fields. Today, for every one acre of cranberry beds, farmers maintain four acres of open wetlands.

41

1820

Maine is separated from Massachusetts in the Missouri Compromise.

IN 1819, MISSOURI APPLIED FOR ADMISSION TO THE Union as the twenty-third state. The move, which threatened to shift the balance of power in favor of those states where slavery was practiced, precipitated a crisis that foreshadowed the Civil War.

The United States at the time of James Monroe's administration resembled a complex chemical equation: a great many volatile elements were delicately balanced to prevent a catastrophic explosion. In the Senate, eleven northern "free states" offset the presence of an equal number of southern "slave states." (The more populous North already controlled the House.)

From the very beginning of the country's history, however, slavery had been a corrosive political element. Slaveholders, who feared that their opponents' zeal might one day rob them of their chattel, repeatedly sought and won protection for what was called the South's "peculiar institution." The rights of slaveholders were duly protected, first in the Constitution and later in federal courts.

In 1787 the Northwest Territory Ordinance barred slavery from all new states north of the Ohio River. The territory of Missouri, a portion of the vast Louisiana Purchase of 1803, lay above that line between the Mississippi and Missouri rivers. In the territory's first decade in American hands, Missouri's sprawling, rich farmlands were rapidly settled by slaveholders from neighboring southern states. Missouri's proposed state constitution, not surprisingly, made slavery legal and permanent.

Abolitionists were not about to allow a new slave state into the Union without a fight. In the House, Rep. James Tallmadge of New York proposed legislation to abolish slavery in Missouri. A debate raged over whether Congress had the authority to make such a law. Eventually Tallmadge's bill passed the House but died in the Senate.

In Massachusetts, the growing influence of abolitionists helped push forward a key element in what became known as the Missouri Compromise. The territory of Maine, which had been part of the commonwealth since early settlement days, applied for admission to the Union as a separate state. In an arrangement backed by Speaker of the House Henry Clay of Kentucky, Maine and Missouri would both be admitted, thus preserving the prevailing balance of senatorial votes and allaying southern fears. Slavery would be banned from the rest of the Louisiana Territory above what is now the northern boundary of Arkansas.

The intense argument that preceded passage of the Missouri Compromise fanned passions on both sides. Thomas Jefferson, a slaveholder himself, wrote that "this momentous question, like a fire-bell in the night, awakened and filled me with terror. I considered it at once as the knell of the Union. It is hushed, indeed, for the moment. But this is a reprieve only, not a final sentence."

42

The Essex is struck by a large sperm whale and sunk.

IN HERMAN MELVILLE'S MASTERPIECE *MOBY-DICK*, an enraged whale demolishes the whaleship *Pequod*. As an inspiration for that climactic scene, literary detectives point to the bizarre cause of the wreck of the *Essex*, a Nantucket whaleship under the command of Capt. George Pollard. At the time of the incident, Melville was a fifteen-month-old infant living in New York City.

On November 20, 1820, after sailing from Nantucket more than a year earlier, the *Essex* lay in the Pacific Ocean just below the equator, a thousand miles due west of Ecuador. With the usual shouts of "There she blows!" sailors sighted a shoal of whales, and two boats were sent into the water. First Mate Owen Chase pursued in one boat, Capt. Pollard in the other. Chase harpooned a whale but was forced to cut his line after the injured creature opened a hole in the boat with its tail.

Chase and his men managed to return to their ship, where they immediately began repairs to the boat in the hope of resuming the chase for the injured leviathan. Suddenly, a sperm whale, which Chase estimated at eighty-five feet long, appeared near the *Essex*. It bore down on the ship at three knots and struck near the bow with its head.

"The ship brought up as suddenly and violently as if she had struck a rock," Chase wrote later. "We looked at each other with perfect amazement, deprived almost of the power of speech." The whale vanished beneath the waves, only to return for a second, even more vicious attack.

Like the smaller boat before it, the *Essex* now began to fill with water from the force of the beast's powerful blows. Pollard and Chase realized quickly enough that pumping was futile. Gathering up bread and water as well as compasses, map books, and other navigation aids, they divided the sailors among three boats.

For three months, the *Essex* sailors drifted in the open sea. They were forced to turn to cannibalism to survive. On Capt. Pollard's boat, which was separated from the others, the men chose lots to determine who should die so that his colleagues might live. In late February the remaining survivors of all three boats were recovered by several passing ships.

Herman Melville did not cross paths with the strange tale of the *Essex* until 1841. As a sailor aboard the *Acushnet* out of New Bedford, he met Owen Chase's son, William Henry Chase. The pair must have enjoyed swapping stories of whaling adventures, and presumably the younger Chase lent Melville a published copy of his father's *Narrative of the Most Extraordinary and Distressing Shipwreck of the Whale-Ship* Essex.

Ten years later, Melville referred to a copy of Chase's *Narrative* when working on his whaling novel. In writing *Moby-Dick*, Melville artfully transformed the *Essex* disaster. No Ahab and no Ishmael figured in Chase's *Narrative*. "Thus, I give up the spear!" is a cry worthy only for literature.

43 | 1825

Unitarianism, first organized in Boston, becomes the unofficial religion of Boston Brahmins.

STRICT PURITAN MORALISM DISSIPATED IN THE commonwealth throughout the eighteenth century as a rising merchant class amassed ever greater wealth. Increasingly, Calvinism proved inconvenient and even unreliable as a philosophical underpinning for international commerce. God's will could not be counted on to provide consistently for substantial profits on all business transactions. Of far greater importance to the bottom line was human will.

Crafty though they became, Boston merchants were not entirely unethical. They gradually lost interest in restrictive religious dogma and theological debates, only to replace them with concerns over conduct and behavior. They often acted out of self-interest, yet they also showed themselves committed to compassion, philanthropy, and social reform. The commonwealth's new merchant class, unlike the Puritans before them, sought converts not to their religious faith but to their moral principles.

In Massachusetts, the drift away from Calvinism accelerated immediately following the end of the Revolutionary War. First to emerge from the fatalistic darkness of Puritanism was Universalism, a new creed transplanted from Europe that optimistically affirmed the ultimate salvation of all. According to Universalism, guilt and punishment for sins were the burdens Jesus accepted on the cross; God would eventually forgive everyone, even Satan and his fallen angels.

In 1780 John Murray, an English immigrant, became minister of the first Universalist congregation in America at Gloucester. The movement eventually coalesced twenty years later around Hosea Ballou, a native of New Hampshire. As author of *Treatise on Atonement* (1805) and later as pastor of Boston's Second Universalist Church, Ballou influenced a generation of Boston intellectuals, including Ralph Waldo Emerson and the Transcendentalists, with his then-radical view of a benevolent God incapable of condemning humanity to eternal punishment.

Congregationalists, the direct theological descendants of the Puritans, faced an internal challenge from liberals within the church at the beginning of the nineteenth century. Leading the attack on Calvinist orthodoxy was William Ellery Channing, minister at Boston's Federal Street Church, who defined a new strain of religious thinking in an 1819 sermon, "Unitarian Christianity." Similar to Universalism, Unitarianism proposed a view of humanity that was positive and affirming and encouraged moral responsibility. In addition, Unitarianism, as the name implies, rejected the doctrine of the Holy Trinity as well as the divinity of Christ.

The American Unitarian Association was formed in Boston in 1825 as an association of individuals, not churches. Channing, Theodore Parker (a well-regarded, free-thinking minister), and others were charter members. Unitarians played a large role in making Boston a center of abolitionism as well as in supporting the city's development as a literary center. "Moral philosophy" classes taught by Harvard College Unitarians also provided the Brahmins with enlightened self-justification.

In the garden cultivated by humanistic Unitarian clergy grew the Boston now remembered as "the Athens of America." Its citizens were serious, prosperous, and thoroughly patrician, yet they managed to be progressive owing to a consistent promotion of public education and private scholarship. "Nothing quieted doubt so completely as the mental calm of the Unitarian clergy," Henry Adams later remembered. "Doubts were a waste of thought. . . . Boston had solved the universe; or had offered and realised the best solution yet tried."

44

1827

The first commercial railroad hauls granite blocks for the Bunker Hill Monument.

OVERLOOKING BOSTON HARBOR IN CHARLESTOWN, the Bunker Hill Monument rises 221 feet and 294 muscle-numbing steps. Like the battle it commemorates, the monument is misnamed; it actually stands on Breed's Hill (Bunker Hill lies not far away and is surmounted by St. Francis Church).

The obelisk of Quincy granite blocks was designed by Solomon Willard, a Boston carpenter-carver turned architect, who had previously worked with the architect-engineer Alexander Parris on St. Paul's Cathedral on Tremont Street. Parris, who built Quincy Market, and Willard were committed practitioners of the Greek Revival movement, then quite popular with Boston Brahmins.

The Bunker Hill Monument Association was founded in 1824 in anticipation of the battle's fiftieth anniversary. Prominent citizens, including

Col. Thomas Handasyd Perkins, a wealthy shipping merchant in the China trade (for whom the Perkins School for the Blind was later named), began a public subscription campaign for the monument's construction. On June 17, 1825, the Marquis de Lafayette, America's great ally in the war for independence, came from France to lay the cornerstone. Another eighteen years would pass, however, before the ambitious building project was completed.

Transporting stone quarried in West Quincy to Charlestown via the Neponset River proved a daunting commercial and technical challenge. Someone suggested that the granite be carried in winter on enormous sledges. A Boston engineer, Gridley Bryant, had a perhaps more practical solution: construction of a railway for horse-drawn carts.

Until this time, single-purpose railways were common enough, but they were never intended as permanent operations. Bryant urged Colonel Perkins and other members of the association to investigate the potential of a permanent commercial railway. On January 5, 1826, the legislature received a petition for the incorporation of the Granite Railway Company.

Construction of such a railway, however, raised many new and provocative questions over such points as right-of-way, safety and liability, and abutters' rights. The legislature very nearly balked at the legal and social tangle involved, but on March 4, 1826, by the thinnest of majorities, they issued the railway a forty-year charter.

Like Francis Cabot Lowell, Bryant was inspired by the example of the English, who had constructed commercial railways for carrying coal from mines, when designing the first such American system. He was compelled to make improvements, nevertheless, particularly in the construction of rails strong enough to accommodate the heavy loads of granite. By 1830 Bryant became frustrated with pine rails and chose to replace them with what was particularly handy for him: granite rails.

On March 27, 1827, the Bunker Hill Monument Association signed a one-year contract for transportation of stone, the first written in the United States for carriage of freight by rail. That spring, the work of hauling granite began. The contract went unrenewed, but the railway was profitable enough with its other business. Wisely, the railway had purchased its own quarry so it would not have to rely on the monument for all its business.

In 1870 the Granite Railway Company was purchased by the Old Colony and Newport Railroad Company. Only then did the new owners replace Bryant's sturdy Quincy granite rails with those made of iron.

45

1829

Dr. Samuel Gridley Howe opens the first school for the blind in the country.

BLINDNESS WAS A COMMON CONDITION IN EARLY nineteenth-century Massachusetts. Diseases, particularly childhood illnesses, frequently robbed people of their sight as well as other senses. Formal education for the blind and deaf did not exist. As a result, the disabled faced limited opportunities for personal development.

In 1784 the first school ever organized exclusively for blind children opened in Paris. Founded by Valentin Hauy, L'Institut National pour Jeunes Aveugles (The National Institute for Blind Youth) pioneered a movement to establish similar schools in Vienna, London, St. Petersburg, Dublin, and elsewhere in Europe. For nearly fifty years, however, no such schools opened across the Atlantic.

Traveling as a medical student, John Fisher of Boston visited Paris in 1826 and toured the National Institute. He met blind students who were learning reading, writing, mathematics, geography, and languages from specially trained teachers. Programs at the French school also included music instruction; blind students were being trained to become church organists. In addition, students printed their own embossed books at an in-school publishing house.

After Fisher returned home to practice medicine, he found the commonwealth's citizens engaged in the first rounds of a vigorous debate over the nature of public education. The young doctor spoke passionately among friends and colleagues on the need for opening up education to the blind.

Finally, in February 1829 at a meeting at Boston's Exchange Coffee House, Fisher organized a group to apply for a private school charter. A year later, the trustees of the New England Asylum for the Blind sent another Boston physician, Samuel Gridley Howe, to tour several European schools for the blind and report on what he saw. (The term *asylum* referred to a haven, or retreat.)

Contrary to Fisher's evangelical enthusiasm following his own tour, Howe returned highly critical of the continent's schools. Raised-type books were in short supply, and other instructional tools were poorly designed. In Howe's view, the students were poorly prepared for life as independent adults. In summary, the European schools were "beacons to warn rather than lights to guide."

The school Howe prepared to open would not be a "retreat" but a stimulating balance of academics, crafts, games, and music. In July 1832 Howe began teaching his first pupils in his father's house; within a month enrollment tripled to six students aged six to twenty. In 1833 Boston merchant Thomas Handasyd Perkins provided his home on Pearl Street for the school's use; the school, now located in Watertown, still bears his name. Supporters held a fund-raising bazaar in Faneuil Hall.

Even as he led the Perkins School for the Blind through its early days, Samuel Gridley Howe served as coeditor of the abolitionist newspaper *The Commonwealth* with his wife, author and women's rights advocate Julia Ward Howe. (In 1862 Julia Ward Howe's poem "The Battle Hymn of the Republic" became a rallying song for Union supporters.)

The Perkins School's most famous student was Helen Keller, an Alabama native who enrolled in 1887. The blind and deaf seven-year-old was patiently taught by Anne Sullivan, herself a Perkins graduate. "We had scarcely arrived at the Perkins School . . . when I began to make friends," Keller wrote in *The Story of My Life*. "I was in my own country." In 1904 Helen Keller graduated cum laude from Radcliffe College, where Sullivan had used a manual alphabet to "spell" the words of the lectures into Helen's hand.

46 | 1831

William Lloyd Garrison begins publishing the abolitionist journal The Liberator.

SON OF A NEWBURYPORT SEAMAN WHO ABANDONED his family, William Lloyd Garrison began adult life as an activist journalist working in Boston and Bennington, Vermont. He gravitated to the emerging abolitionist movement as a convert from the American Colonization Society, which urged the peaceful repatriation of slaves to Africa. Instead, Garrison and others favored "immediatism," the immediate emancipation of slaves and their assimilation into American life.

In 1830, two million slaves lived in the territory of the United States. Their contribution to the young country's growing wealth was perhaps incalculable, but slave auctioneers were expected to get the highest possible price. A field hand in his prime who could pick 150 pounds of cotton in a single day fetched about $1,300 on the block in New Orleans's busy slave market.

The South's "peculiar institution"—then protected by the U.S. Constitution—demanded and received a surprising degree of respect. Few dared to challenge slavery or slaveholders with any vehemence. This changed dramatically in 1831: in Virginia, Nat Turner led a slave insurrection, and in Boston, William Lloyd Garrison published *The Liberator,* the first abolitionist newspaper.

Several weeks after Turner's rebellion was put down, Garrison warned prophetically that worse was to come: "The first drops of blood, which are but the prelude to a deluge from the gathering clouds, have fallen," he declared in an editorial. He termed the U.S. Constitution "an agreement with hell" and set a copy alight at a Framingham rally. Garrison relished the uproar his words and actions caused among southern slaveholders and northern sympathizers. "If those who deserve the lash feel it and wince at it," he wrote, "I shall be assured I am striking the right persons in the right place."

Statue of William Lloyd Garrison

Until the Civil War's end, Garrison agitated for abolition as fervently as anyone in the United States. He saw a parallel in the slaves' fight for freedom with another uprising against tyranny.

"Rather than see men wearing their chains in a cowardly and servile spirit, I would, as an advocate of peace, much rather see them breaking the head of the tyrant with their chains," Garrison told a Boston audience in December 1859. "Give me, as a nonresistant, Bunker Hill, and Lexington, and Concord, rather than the cowardice and servility of a southern slave plantation."

47

Mount Auburn Cemetery, the nation's first "garden cemetery," opens in Cambridge.

AS A REFORM MOVEMENT AMONG MANY THEN thriving in Boston, burial reform was hardly as incendiary as calls for abolition of slavery; as ponderous as the recently concluded drive to establish a municipal form of government; or as fundamental to existence as the possible construction of a public water reservoir.

Nevertheless, burial reform managed to capture the public's attention throughout the 1820s. Debate raged in Boston over how best to address the urban dilemma of rapidly diminishing burial space.

This housing crisis for the dead was a direct result of the tripling of Boston's population in the generation since the end of the Revolutionary War. Ensuring proper sanitation and healthful living conditions for all citizens became a new concern. Civic leaders faulted Boston's narrow, winding streets for encouraging disease, while they encouraged development of the Back Bay, an odoriferous swamp.

Overcrowding in the city's cemeteries was not entirely a new concern. The King's Chapel, Copp's Hill, and Old Granary Burying Grounds were already reaching capacity as early as 1730. A fourth burying ground was opened in 1756 and another in 1810, for a total burial space of fewer than five acres. A new interment was likely to unearth remains of coffins and bones from previous burials. Grave robbers (called "resurrection men") harvested cadavers for local physicians from the bumper crop of corpses. Health concerns eventually led to calls for a ban on cattle grazing in cemeteries.

The lot fell to a man named, remarkably, Coffin to set burial reform in motion. On July 4, 1823, Dr. John Gorham Coffin, a highly regarded physician, published a pamphlet arguing that urban burying grounds led to disease fostered by putrefaction. He called for creation of a sprawling

suburban cemetery where bodies might decompose quickly and without exposing city inhabitants to danger from unhealthful air. This new grave-yard would not be located near a church; instead, nature would provide the reposeful setting.

Another physician, Dr. Jacob Bigelow, took up Coffin's argument with great enthusiasm. A professor of medicine at Harvard as well as a botanist, Bigelow eventually persuaded George Brimmer, who had assembled a seventy-two-acre lot in rural Cambridge and Watertown, to sell his large holding at cost to the Massachusetts Horticultural Society. As proprietors of the first rural cemetery in the United States, the society began selling family burial lots in June 1831. For the cemetery's name, Dr. Bigelow recast a common nickname Harvard students had given the area. "Sweet Auburn" became "Mount Auburn."

Within a relatively brief time after its opening, Mount Auburn Cemetery became well known as the final resting place for some of Boston and Cambridge's most famous names. Henry Wadsworth Longfellow, Charles Bulfinch, Harrison Gray Otis, Isabella Stewart Gardner, and Winslow Homer are among the many notables. A thoughtful landscaping plan of shady trees and flowering plants also attracted many who simply wanted to take a stroll in a relaxing atmosphere. Mount Auburn thus played an important inspirational role in the nineteenth-century movement to create urban public parks. It now has more than eighty-six thousand permanent residents—and is still a favorite destination for long walks.

48

1837

Horace Mann oversees creation of the first state board of education.

IN THE EARLY NINETEENTH CENTURY, MASSACHUSETTS could boast of a long-standing tradition of support for public education. It was the home to the nation's oldest public school, Boston Latin (founded in 1635), and state laws mandating publicly funded education were already two centuries old. Yet Horace Mann was not impressed. The brilliant president of the Massachusetts Senate was a determined social reformer with an incisive legal mind and great oratorical skill. In 1833 he helped establish a state hospital in Worcester for the mentally ill, the first of its kind in the United States. (The hospital was later dubbed, respectfully, "Mann's Monument.")

Next, Mann turned to the commonwealth's schools. "Men are cast-iron; but children are wax," he wrote, averring that education has tremendous power to shape the future. The crusading Mann found the prevailing conditions in public schools to be a public disgrace. Bare walls, no maps, a few books, and a switch to keep some semblance of discipline were the typical schoolmaster's only materials. A class of fifteen students might be crammed into a fourteen-by-eighteen-foot space. An outhouse was a luxury that students and schoolmaster alike lived without. Public school teachers such as Henry David Thoreau in Concord and Herman Melville in a rural school near Pittsfield gave up their positions rather than continue in what they considered a form of servitude.

Massachusetts parents showed little concern for improving the schools, and town officials showed even less desire to pay for any improvements. The state government, Mann and others realized, must step into the breach.

In 1837, Mann, acting as the president of the Senate, was at the head of the push to establish a state board of education, the first of its kind in the nation. Supporters believed that the new agency, although advisory in nature, would spur a movement for much-needed reforms. The board's first members, including Governor Edward Everett, convinced Mann that only he was qualified to serve as its first secretary. He accepted, knowing that he would have to relinquish, or at least suspend indefinitely, a promising political career.

In eleven years as secretary of the board, Mann gained national prominence and exerted a lasting influence on the public conception of education. Among the principles he firmly established were that public education must be sectarian and free of religious dogma; that all children, regardless of their background, must be educated equally; and that only a professional cadre of teachers can deliver a worthy education.

Such tenets hardly seem debatable today, yet they upset many Massachusetts residents in the 1840s. Clergymen thought sectarian schools would promote atheism. Local officials were offended that Mann and the state government should try to usurp their authority. Mann, a progressive knight, was undeterred from his crusade for educational reform. He later became the first president of Antioch College, in Yellow Springs, Ohio, which was dedicated to providing a university education regardless of race, creed, or sex.

49

Mary Lyon founds Mount Holyoke College, the nation's first college for women.

WHEN MARY LYON DIED IN 1849 AT THE AGE OF fifty-two, she had seen more than sixteen hundred young women pass through the doors of the Mount Holyoke Female Seminary in the dozen years since she helped to found the school. Along with teachers and foreign missionaries (occupations that nineteenth-century women often found themselves confined to), Mount Holyoke's early graduates included some of the nation's first women doctors.

Mary Lyon was born in 1797 on a country farm in Buckland, Massachusetts. At the time, the western portion of the commonwealth was already becoming a popular retreat for American and European travelers, who leisurely followed a well-worn stagecoach route from Boston to New York via Springfield, Hartford, and New Haven. These mostly urban visitors enjoyed the gentle landscapes of the Connecticut River Valley and appreciated the quiet charms of rural New England.

At seventeen, Mary Lyon began her first teaching job in Buckland's one-room schoolhouse. In 1821 she received important training at Rev. Joseph Emerson's school for teachers in Byfield, north of Boston near Newburyport. Lyon was quickly recognized for her teaching abilities and her commitment to education. She was soon appointed "preceptress" at Sanderson Academy, Ashfield, nearer her childhood home.

The region north of Springfield had changed dramatically since Mary Lyon was a girl. By the 1830s, "Canal Village" at South Hadley Falls was a booming factory town with two woolen mills, three paper mills, two pearl button factories, and a linseed oil–processing plant—which together employed hundreds of men and women. Local landowners, mill bosses, and merchants were determined to see their young daughters receive what was then called a "seminary" education. In 1834 seven such men gathered in

Mount Holyoke College

Mary Lyon's home after she circulated a plan for such a school, the New England Seminary for Teachers.

In January 1835 South Hadley's citizens voted to support the new school with an $8,000 subscription, helping to lure Lyon and her colleagues away from establishing it in either Sunderland or South Deerfield. By all accounts, Mary Lyon was an especially capable fund-raiser, even in the face of a national economic depression. She traveled frequently and could persuade wealthy businessmen and ladies' sewing circles to support the school. Individual donations given toward the endowment ranged from six cents to $1,000.

A four-story school building accommodating eighty students was ready at last on November 8, 1837. According to a schedule prepared by Mary Lyon, the first school bells rang at 4:00 A.M. and the last at 10:00 P.M. For health reasons, all students were required to walk a mile a day.

"Go where no one else will go," Lyon urged her students. "Do what no one else will do."

In addition to classroom education, the founder of Mount Holyoke emphasized a "domestic plan" of study that required students to do much of the school's housekeeping. The effort involved, she believed, would help to build young character (and save on administrative costs). Well respected for her thrift, Lyon was notorious for paying teachers poorly. She defended herself by calling the school "a family." To her credit, Lyon maintained a policy of keeping tuition and boarding costs as low as possible in order to admit the daughters of middle-class families.

50

1840

Margaret Fuller is appointed editor of The Dial, a new journal of transcendental thought.

EVERYONE IN THE TRANSCENDENTALIST CLUB wanted to see the group publish a literary journal, but no one wanted to serve as the editor. Reformists of worldly and otherwordly institutions, the Transcendentalists were eager to spread word of their new ideas for education, women's rights, and social change well beyond their home base in Concord. As the group's founder, Ralph Waldo Emerson must have felt pressure to take up the task, but he instead turned to his friend Margaret Fuller and proposed the idea to her.

As editor of *The Dial*, Margaret Fuller enjoyed the privilege of wresting prose and poetry contributions from Emerson as well as from Henry Thoreau, Bronson Alcott, Theodore Parker, and Elizabeth Peabody, among other New England writers and philosophers. When she found herself short of copy, Fuller filled out *The Dial* with her own work. Her sentimental article

"The Great Composers" is less absorbing today than "The Great Lawsuit: Man vs. Men, Woman vs. Women," a farsighted expression of radical feminism. In it, Fuller dared to declare equality for women as an inalienable right. "We would have every path laid open to women as freely as to man," she wrote firmly.

Few who knew Fuller would have found anything surprising in "The Great Lawsuit." As a child, she received the same rigorous education as her brothers. Timothy Fuller, a stern but loving father, imbued young Margaret with high standards and an ambition for intellectual achievement. Later, he demanded of an awkward teenager that she also learn proper social manners. As a result, a combination of intellectual ability and personal warmth prepared Margaret Fuller for a controversial life as, arguably, America's first feminist.

Throughout her twenties, Fuller taught at Bronson Alcott's Temple School in Boston and in Providence; she published a translation of J. P. Eckermann's *Conversations with Goethe* and began (but never completed) a biography of the German author. She became a favorite of the Transcendentalists who gathered for conversation at Elizabeth Palmer Peabody's bookstore on West Street in Boston.

With encouragement from her friends, Fuller, then twenty-nine, undertook a series of ten "Conversations" with women in the winter of 1839. She charged $20 for the unusual programs, which were conducted in a pedagogical method in the form of exchanges with students. Fuller chose topics ranging from the fine arts and mythology to prudence and health. Men were forbidden to attend the sessions. Fuller believed that by leading only women in intellectual conversation, she might spark a feminist revolution. Her goal was nothing less than sexual equality. The "Conversations" proved so successful that she continued to offer them for five years.

Fuller faced accusations common to women who challenge the authority of men. She was vain, some people said, or arrogant. Her male friends criticized her as artificial or sentimental. Nevertheless, Fuller was capable of declaring, apparently without irony, "I now know all the people worth knowing in America, and I find no intellect comparable to my own."

51 | 1841

George and Sophia Ripley create the Brook Farm Institute of Agriculture and Education.

RALPH WALDO EMERSON WAS PERHAPS TOO MUCH an individualist in the first place, but what seems decisively to have prevented the high priest of transcendentalism from living at Brook Farm was the community's unorthodox system of delegating work and paying wages.

Under Brook Farm's bylaws, its members were free to choose their tasks and to start and stop work as they pleased, all according to each person's conscience. They were also paid at exactly the same rate—ten cents an hour—for whatever work they performed, menial or intellectual, from shoveling dirt to writing a poem.

Emerson preferred the discipline and common sense of the Protestant work ethic, which compensated according to skill and effort applied. In this opinion, he was joined by a Concord neighbor, a farmer who told Emerson he thought the Brook Farm methods so impractical that if he followed them, he would wind up very shortly in the poorhouse.

"It was a perpetual picnic," the philosopher observed after one of several Brook Farm visits, "a French Revolution in small; an Age of Reason in a patty-pan."

Certainly, Brook Farm (located in what is now West Roxbury) was all those things, though in a way that Emerson could not conceive—that was the whole point. The community's original members lived together in a farmhouse they called "The Hive." They did not intend to start a profitable business, but they did plan to support themselves by running a farm and school. Like revolutionaries, they wanted to overthrow royalty—in this case, the Yankee King Lucre and its consort, Materialism. In their place, the Brook Farm members would establish a new society of love and harmony.

Such an idealistic living experiment is usually called a utopian community, after Sir Thomas More's sixteenth-century essay about a perfect society called Utopia. The term *utopian*, however, can describe any idealistic social venture. George and Sophia Ripley, who founded the Brook Farm Institute of Agriculture and Education in April 1841, were aware of the failures of past Utopias. In businesslike fashion, they financed their experimental community by selling shares of stock at $500 each. To augment any farm income, the Ripleys opened several schools at the site. The Brook Farm School was soon well attended and praised for its efforts to "perfect freedom of relations between students and teaching body."

With its communal living arrangements and liberal philosophy of individual freedom, Brook Farm naturally attracted conservative criticism. Despite rumors of promiscuous behavior among residents, Brook Farm was essentially a religious community, founded on a footloose interpretation of New England's own religion, Unitarianism. The community was set apart from the venal world much as the first Puritan settlements had been.

Among the original shareholders was Nathaniel Hawthorne, though the author found communal living not to his liking and left Brook Farm after just six months. Brook Farm members organized concerts, poetry readings, and other entertainments for themselves and their guests. Frequent if not always entirely sympathetic visitors included Emerson as well as his transcendentalist colleague Margaret Fuller; abolitionist Theodore Parker; and Bronson Alcott (the father of Louisa May Alcott), who in 1843 organized a similar community, Fruitlands, at Harvard, Massachusetts.

To the Ripleys' credit, Brook Farm defied its critics and prospered for several years. In 1844 the community had grown to 120 members and had adopted the theories of Charles Fourier, a radical French philosopher and early socialist. Its members decided to build what they called a "phalanstery," an enormous building planned to include suites of living quarters for entire families as well as a dining room seating three hundred. After two years of work, on March 3, 1846, the phalanstery, almost completed but not yet occupied, burned to the ground. The Brook Farm community never recovered from the catastrophe.

A further blow came four days after the fire, when Middlesex County Court in Cambridge heard the case of *Nathaniel Hawthorne v. George Ripley et al.* and found in favor of the plaintiff. Hawthorne had sued for return of his

$500 investment in Brook Farm and won a judgment of $560.62, including legal expenses. To add insult to civil injury, the writer later wrote a stinging satire of his Brook Farm days, *The Blithedale Romance*.

Utopian communities such as Brook Farm are individually recollected as failures, yet taken together they represent the highest aspirations of all human communities, The high-minded settlement on a then-semirural stretch of the Charles River boosted American cultural development by expanding the native notions of liberty beyond the political to include the personal.

52

1841

Frederick Douglass, an escaped slave, gives his first public speech on Nantucket.

IN THE SUMMER OF 1841, FREDERICK DOUGLASS set out from his adopted home in New Bedford for a sojourn on Nantucket, where abolitionists were gathering for the first Anti-Slavery Convention. "I have had no holiday since establishing myself in New Bedford," he wrote, "and, feeling the need of a little rest, I determined to attend the meeting, though I have no thought of taking any part in the proceedings."

It was not precisely a vacation, but the five days he spent on the island profoundly transformed Douglass in the way we often hope that time spent away from our ordinary occupations may change us for the better. Three years after escaping bondage in his native Maryland, he left the New Bedford wharves a shipyard laborer and returned to them an inspiring orator in the cause to end slavery.

That Nantucket should be the setting for such a rebirth is little wonder. Influenced by the libertarian values of a large Quaker community, the island was an established sanctuary for escaped slaves. Nantucket's small but proud African American community was known as "Guiney" or "New Guinea." Prosperous "Guiney" Nantucketers included Absalom Boston, a whaling captain and real estate investor, and the prominent Godrey and Harris families.

In the Five Corners section of Nantucket Town, Guiney community members gathered at the African Meeting House for church and meetings. Nantucket's Native Americans and Cape Verdean immigrants also were welcomed. The Meeting House, which remains standing, was used as a school for the island's minority children until all Nantucket schools became integrated in 1846.

With forty other white and black abolitionists, Douglass boarded the steamboat *Telegraph* bound for Nantucket, only to learn from its captain that the ship would not leave unless all the black passengers took quarters separate from the whites. The convention delegates flatly refused, but eventually they reached a compromise: all would remain exclusively on the boat's upper deck. Once under way, the abolitionists held a protest meeting against the ferry company's segregationist practices.

Waiting to meet Douglass at the Nantucket dock was William Coffin, a New Bedford bookkeeper and abolitionist who had earlier heard the escaped slave speak at a black assembly. The sight of the two men walking together through the streets of Nantucket Town defied unwritten codes maintaining strict racial separation. Undeterred, Coffin planted the suggestion with Douglass that he should speak during the next day's meetings.

In his autobiography, *Narrative of the Life of Frederick Douglass, an American Slave, Written by Himself* (published in Boston by the Anti-Slavery Office in 1845), Douglass recalled the emotional moment of his first speech, August 9, 1841. "The truth was, I felt myself a slave," he wrote, "and the idea of speaking to white people weighed me down. I spoke but a few moments, when I felt a degree of freedom, and said what I desired with considerable ease. . . . I trembled in every limb." Those few moments inaugurated a career in public life that spanned the remainder of the nineteenth century, and which would ultimately take Douglass to the White House, where he discussed with Lincoln the recruitment of freed slaves to the Union Army, and later, to Port-au-Prince, Haiti, where Douglass served as the U.S. ambassador.

William Lloyd Garrison's recollection of the address his friend gave was considerably less modest: "In the course of his speech [he] gave utterance to many noble thoughts and thrilling recollections," the publisher of *The Liberator* recounted. "I rose, and declared that Patrick Henry, of revolutionary fame, never made a speech more eloquent in the cause of liberty, than the one we had just listened to." Turning to the audience, Garrison then demanded, "Shall such a man ever be sent back to slavery from the soil of old Massachusetts?"

The replies of "No!" and "Never!" were said to shake the walls and roof of the Nantucket Atheneum.

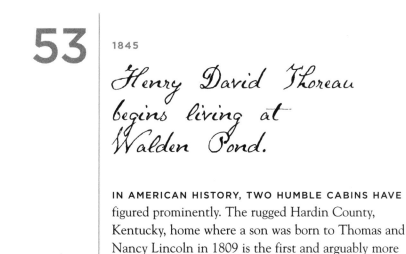

53 | 1845

Henry David Thoreau begins living at Walden Pond.

IN AMERICAN HISTORY, TWO HUMBLE CABINS HAVE figured prominently. The rugged Hardin County, Kentucky, home where a son was born to Thomas and Nancy Lincoln in 1809 is the first and arguably more famous. The simple Concord shack where an eccentric Harvard graduate purposefully lived a self-sufficient existence beginning in 1845 is the other.

Few writers have ever made more of their own idiosyncratic behavior than Henry David Thoreau. He could shape a point of principle from his smallest quirk. (A determined shirker, he famously warned, "Beware all enterprises that require new clothes.") In this way Thoreau achieved a kind of offbeat heroism that owes nothing to achievement or victory and everything to strength of inner character. "The greater part of what my neighbors call good I believe in my soul to be bad," wrote Thoreau, "and if I repent of anything it is very likely to be my good behavior."

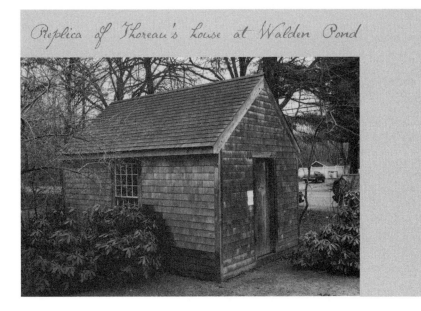

Replica of Thoreau's House at Walden Pond

Throughout his relatively short life (he died in 1862 when not quite forty-five years old), Thoreau irritated his companions and his neighbors in the same fashion as Jesus or Socrates. He was an insufferable scold and clearly enjoyed the role. In an age when the burgeoning railroad symbolized a nation's boundless ambition for wealth, territory, and power, Thoreau observed pointedly, "We do not ride on the railroad; it rides upon us."

Shortly after his Harvard College graduation, Thoreau met Ralph Waldo Emerson, a fellow citizen of Concord. At Emerson's suggestion, Thoreau began a diary. He also took up writing poetry, a profession that meagerly supported him for most of the 1840s. With his brother John for company, Thoreau made a canoe trip along the Concord and Merrimack rivers in 1838 and soon began turning out essays on his experiences in nature. Among these was "Natural History of Massachusetts," which Margaret Fuller published in *The Dial* in 1842. *A Week on the Concord and Merrimack Rivers* appeared in 1849 but sold only 220 copies.

In 1845 Thoreau decided to build a cabin at Emerson's estate at Walden Pond. He declared his intention plainly: "I went to the woods because I wished to live deliberately, to front only the essential facts of life, and see if I could not learn what it had to teach, and not, when I came to die, discover that I had not lived."

While living at Walden Pond, Thoreau was arrested by Sam Staples, Concord's constable and tax gatherer. As a protest against slavery and the conduct of the Mexican-American War, Thoreau had persistently refused to pay his poll tax. He was released after a single night in the town jail, however, when an unknown woman, most likely his aunt, paid the tax for him. Thoreau drew on the experience for his most influential essay, "Civil Disobedience," in which he defended the right of the individual to refuse to comply with the unjust rule of a majority.

When he finally abandoned his cabin at Walden on September 6, 1847, Thoreau was a deeply changed man. He spent the remaining fifteen years of his life apparently reconciled with the contradictory nature of his soul. He became a surveyor, and when his father died, he managed the family's pencil-making business in Concord. Thoreau continued to travel and wrote warmly of his trips to Maine, Cape Cod, and Canada. He also became an ardent abolitionist.

Walden was published in 1854, the second and last of his books published in his lifetime. It took him five years to sell the two thousand copies printed.

54

1846

The first operation under anesthesia is performed at Massachusetts General Hospital.

BEFORE THE NINETEENTH CENTURY, THE HISTORY of surgery was inextricably linked to the search for a reliable general "anesthetic" (from the Greek word for "absence of sensation"). Ever since God caused a deep sleep to fall on Adam before the legendary chest operation that created Eve, physicians had longed for a method to dull their patients' senses. Brandy, opium, laudanum, and mandrake root could

provide some pain relief and even induce unconsciousness, but results varied widely. Early narcotics were ingested before surgery. Once administered, the drugs could not be controlled. Supposedly senseless patients often felt pain; complications frequently arose during operations; many patients died.

In 1799 English scientist Sir Humphrey Davy noted that inhaling nitrous oxide, which he called "laughing gas," relieved pain. He also pointed out that only through the lungs may a drug be withdrawn as easily as it is given. Sir Humphrey pointedly suggested that laughing gas be used in surgery.

Davy's pupil Michael Faraday carried this line of research further and discovered the pain-relieving qualities of ether, a colorless, volatile, organic liquid. In time, both laughing gas and ether became popular as intoxicants. Surgeons, however, remained uninterested in any potential medical use until a demonstration of the peculiar properties of laughing gas inspired a Connecticut dentist, Horace Wells, to conduct an unusual experiment in 1844. While Dr. Wells inhaled nitrous oxide, his pupil, William Thomas Green Morton, painlessly extracted one of the dentist's own teeth.

Traveling to Boston and Massachusetts General Hospital, Dr. Morton persuaded Dr. John C. Warren, the hospital's cofounder, to attempt an operation using ether as a general anesthetic.

On October 16, 1846, in the amphitheater of the hospital's main building (designed by Charles Bulfinch, and still standing), Dr. Warren operated on Gilbert Abbott for removal of a tumor on the jaw while Dr. Morton administered the ether with a device he had designed. Afterward Abbott declared, "I have felt no pain," and Dr. Warren endorsed the procedure with the remark, "Gentlemen, this is no humbug."

Within a year of that successful operation, ether was being used worldwide to relieve the pain of surgery. The Massachusetts General amphitheater quickly became known as "the Ether Dome."

Several other physicians claimed to have used ether as a general anesthetic before the sensational Massachusetts General demonstration. Dr. Morton became involved in a lengthy feud with his former housemate, Dr. Charles T. Jackson, a doctor and chemist from whom Morton learned much about ether's characteristics.

Thus, when it came time to dedicate a monument to the discovery in the Public Garden, sculptor John Quincy Adams Ward faced a quandary: whom, exactly, should he honor? He wisely chose to omit names altogether and honor only the discovery itself. At this diplomatic sleight of hand, Oliver Wendell Holmes quipped that the monument was "a memorial to ether— or to either."

Located near the Public Garden's Commonwealth Avenue entrance, the Ether Monument rises from a base of lion-headed spouts surmounted by arches and columns to support figures of the Good Samaritan comforting a suffering youth.

55

The first national Woman's Rights Convention convenes in Worcester.

A NEWSPAPER REPORTER ASSIGNED TO COVER THE two days of speeches and caucuses decided he could see right through the whole affair. "The whole purpose of the convention was too apparent for concealment," he wrote. "It is *but a new form of antislavery agitation*" (italics in original).

The journalist for the *Worcester Palladium* had only noted the obvious. In attendance at the first national Woman's Rights Convention, held at Worcester's Brinley Hall on October 23 and 24, 1850, were such abolitionist luminaries as Frederick Douglass and William Lloyd Garrison, as well as famed Quaker activist Lucretia Mott and eleven hundred male and female delegates from eleven states. From the basic proposition that the slaves should be freed, the abolitionists reasoned, it followed immediately that women must be liberated, too.

A year earlier in the abolitionist newspaper *The Liberator* (see page 81), William Lloyd Garrison made the point when he called for women's suffrage, a thoroughly radical notion. His abolitionist colleague Wendell Phillips concurred and boldly described the Women's Rights Convention as "the first organized protest against the injustice which has brooded over the character and destiny of one half the human race."

In the published "call" for the convention, the language was similarly reminiscent of abolitionist tracts. Promoters denounced "the tyranny which degrades and crushes wives and mothers" and noted further, "Woman has been condemned, for greater delicacy of physical organization, to inferiority of intellectual and moral culture and the forfeiture of great social, civil and religious privileges. In the relation of marriage, she has been ideally annihilated, and actually enslaved in all that concerns her personal and pecuniary right."

One delegate even chose to illustrate the parallel of conditions for women and blacks with a harrowing story of the sort abolitionists never tired of telling. While traveling in Europe, the delegate testified, she witnessed a woman and a cow yoked together and dragging a plow while her husband walked behind and drove the team.

Worcester and the surrounding central Massachusetts region had become a hotbed for women's rights advocates. Convention delegates Abby Kelley and Stephen Foster (the abolitionist, not the songwriter), for example, had married themselves in Worcester in 1845 with vows that pointedly left out the traditional promise for a wife to obey her husband. The Fosters scrupulously divided the chores in the household, and when a daughter was born, Stephen remained at home on their farm while Abby, a former schoolteacher who had been inspired by Garrison to take up the cause of abolition as well as women's rights, traveled the lecture circuit.

At the second national Women's Rights Convention, a year later, Abby Kelley Foster challenged the other delegates "not to go home to complain of the men." A few of them may have muttered under their breath that their men were no Stephen Fosters.

56

1854

Runaway slave Anthony Burns is captured in Boston under the Fugitive Slave Act.

THE ARREST OF A TWENTY-YEAR-OLD AFRICAN American on a trumped-up burglary charge set Boston on edge in May 1854. Both black and white Bostonians were united in common concern for the fate of Anthony Burns, the property of Col. Charles Suttle of Stafford County, Virginia.

As part of the Compromise of 1850, a bitterly divided Congress had balanced the entry of California to the Union as a free state with the passage of a strict Fugitive Slave Act that made it easier for southern slaveholders to recover runaways. Federal commissioners were authorized to seize and try any suspected escaped slaves without allowing them to testify at trial and without a jury. The commissioner received a double fee if he ruled the suspect a runaway slave rather than legally free.

For four years the new law had quietly terrorized the commonwealth's black community, which included several hundred escaped slaves. Among them was Anthony Burns, who stowed away on a northbound ship in February 1854 and found work at a Boston clothing store. After locating his slave through a letter Burns wrote home to his brother, Colonel Suttle demanded his rights under the Fugitive Slave Act. Fearful black Bostonians took to carrying weapons to protect themselves against any further attacks by zealous agents. Even the ordinarily pacifistic Frederick Douglass defended the use of violence in an editorial for *The Liberator*, asking rhetorically, "Is It Right and Wise to Kill a Kidnapper?"

At Faneuil Hall, a multiracial protest attracted what is thought to have been the largest assembly ever in that famous meeting place. It was easily the most furious crowd ever. Abolitionist orator Theodore Parker let the sarcasm drip from his lips. "Fellow subjects of Virginia!" he addressed the crowd. Even as the Bostonians listening shouted, "No!" Parker applied salt to the wound. "There was a Boston once," he declared. "Now there is a north suburb to the city of Alexandria."

In a short time, the excited audience no longer bothered to listen to Parker. He had greatly provoked them, and when it was proposed that the protest continue the next morning at the courthouse where Burns was being held, the people were clearly not in the mood to wait. "Tonight! Tonight!" they chanted.

Even as the crowd surged out of Faneuil Hall into the night, a volunteer team of blacks and whites assembled by the abolitionist Vigilance Committee hammered at the courthouse door with a battering ram. Guards armed with cutlasses repelled the attack, but not before one guard fell dead. Reinforcements arrived in time to hold back the Faneuil Hall crowd. "It was one of the best plots that ever failed," remembered one of the organizers. Thirteen were arrested but later freed. No one was ever indicted in the guard's murder.

Legal arguments on Burns's behalf equally failed. On June 2 he was led through the streets to a boat waiting at Long Wharf. The parade route was lined with people, but there was no violence. Buildings were draped in mourning, and American flags were flown upside down. A coffin labeled "Liberty" lay in state outside Old South Church.

After his return to Virginia in 1855, Anthony Burns regained his freedom. Rev. Leonard Grimes, pastor of Boston's Twelfth Baptist Church, where Burns had worshiped, raised $1,300, Suttle's price for his slave, plus expenses. A year earlier, Grimes had offered Suttle $1,200 for Burns's freedom but was refused, not by the colonel, but by a federal agent who stood to make a handsome fee if the slave was successfully returned.

57

1858

The filling of the Back Bay begins.

ENVIRONMENTAL REGULATIONS TODAY MAKE THE draining and filling of wetlands difficult, if not impossible. In the 1850s, however, no such regulations existed to thwart city and state officials, working in a consortium with private landowners, from filling in the area of Boston now known as the Back Bay. The massive landfill project was even something of an environmental boon, as it cleaned up a foul-smelling and unsightly 580-acre public dump and gave the city the Commonwealth Avenue mall.

The Shawmut peninsula, which became the site of the first European settlements of Boston, resembled a cut flower lying on its side in Boston Harbor. Its stem, a narrow natural causeway, was known as Boston Neck and roughly followed what is today Washington Street. The Charles River estuary surrounded the roughly circular blossom of the flower to the west and south. In these tidal marshes, Native Americans constructed fishing weirs thousands of years ago. The same marshes ran up to the edge of Boston Common and presented early Bostonians with a featureless, if not unappealing, backyard view.

Visionaries, though, could see the development possibilities in the Back Bay from as early as the end of the eighteenth century. In the first decades after independence, Boston grew to bursting size as available land was strained to hold a burgeoning population.

Boston accommodated its growth with vigorous action. In 1804 the town annexed Dorchester Neck. Mill Pond, an artificial body of water formed by a seventeenth-century landfill scheme at the mouth of the Charles River, was ordered to be filled with land scooped from the side of Beacon Hill. Today, North Station and Massachusetts General Hospital sit on this fill.

In 1813 a Boston town meeting approved construction of Mill Dam and Turnpike Road, which extended Beacon Street past Boston Common and followed a line across the northern edge of the Back Bay. Mills in South Boston would operate with power from tidal waters rushing through the dam.

As an inevitable consequence of the dam's construction, however, the Back Bay was drained every day. The land was exposed to the sun and other elements that promote unhealthy organic decay. In addition, Bostonians were unable to resist the human urge to dump garbage and other waste where they believed no one would notice it. But people did take horrified notice: the odor, the putrefaction, and the rats were appalling.

The first improvement made in the Back Bay was development of the Public Garden on land beyond Boston Common, beginning in 1839. The city's attention soon was drawn to the remaining land in the Back Bay as a site for real estate speculation. In 1849 the area was conveniently declared a health hazard, and a committee was appointed to determine a solution. Elected officials, property owners, and amateur city planners responded with fantasy-filled designs that included Elysian Fields, Silver Lake, grand boulevards in the French style, even circus grounds on an island in the Charles.

In 1857 the commissioners on the Back Bay finally approved a grandiose development plan. Commonwealth Avenue, two hundred feet wide, was to run west from Arlington Street at the Public Garden, with Newbury and Marlborough streets lying south and north, respectively. Beacon and Boylston streets were extended west along their existing paths.

Within a year the state contracted for removal of land from Pemberton Hill as well as for the hauling of gravel by railroad from Needham. The commonwealth paid for the ambitious project by the sale of developable lots. In 1859 a journalist described trains up to thirty-five cars long, each one loaded with gravel and other landfill material, arriving in the Back Bay every forty-five minutes, day and night.

Among the first of Boston's elite to move into the Back Bay were Mr. and Mrs. John L. Gardner, who were married in 1859. As a wedding gift from her father, Isabella Stewart and her new husband received the lot for 152 Beacon Street, where they built a four-story mansion in 1862. Major construction work continued in the Back Bay well into the 1880s. Perhaps the musicians playing in Mrs. Gardner's Parisian-style drawing room helped to drown out the trundling sound of gravel trains and the din of pile drivers.

58

Milton Bradley publishes a board game, "The Checkered Game of Life."

IN A SMALL OFFICE OPPOSITE COURT SQUARE IN Springfield in 1860, Milton Bradley and his business partner, William Child, installed a used lithographic press. Lithography was still a recent printing innovation, and the press was the only one of its kind in the state outside Boston.

The Milton Bradley Company, Publishers & Lithographers, had a quick if unlikely hit with a full-color print of Abraham Lincoln of Illinois, the popular 1860 Republican presidential candidate. When Lincoln grew a beard following his election, a hapless Bradley was suddenly left with an obsolete product. A more consistent seller over time proved to be a board game, "The Checkered Game of Life," which the printer invented and which he introduced in 1860.

The rise of Bradley's career as a creator of board games and other home entertainments coincided with the development of a revolutionary new educational philosophy. German educator Friedrich Froebel had recently invented what he called *kindergarten*, based on his theories that children learn best through creative play. Froebel also started his own publishing firm for play and educational books. Spurred on by Elizabeth Peabody of Massachusetts, a pioneer in child education, Milton Bradley adopted the Froebelian idea that learning should be fun.

Now based in East Longmeadow, the Milton Bradley Company (which was purchased by Hasbro in 1984) is the largest and oldest game manufacturer in the world.

59

1863

Col. Robert Gould Shaw leads the nation's first African American regiment.

IN MARCH 1863, FREDERICK DOUGLASS STRONGLY declared his pride in the example Massachusetts had set for the nation in the cause of liberty and racial equality. "She was the first in the War of Independence; first to break the chains of her slaves; first to make the black man equal before the law; first to admit colored children to her common schools," the former slave noted as he exhorted other former slaves to enlist in the Union Army's first black regiment.

"Massachusetts now welcomes you to arms as soldiers," he continued. "This is our golden opportunity. Let us accept it, and forever wipe out the dark reproaches unsparingly hurled against us by our enemies. Let us win for ourselves the gratitude of our country, and the best blessings of our prosperity through all time."

The regiment that marched through downtown Boston on May 28, 1863, toward troop ships waiting at Battery Wharf included Charles and Lewis Douglass, the great orator's own sons, as well as hundreds of free Massachusetts blacks and fugitive slaves who had returned from safety in Canada. The soldiers ceremoniously marched past the spot near the Old State House where Crispus Attucks had fallen dead in the Boston Massacre. For the first time in American history, African Americans were formally allowed to fight for their country.

As commander of the 54th, Col. Robert Gould Shaw, twenty-five, made a handsome, sword-bearing symbol of the strength of abolitionist sentiment in Massachusetts. Shaw was raised on Beacon Hill in a white family who regarded abolition as seriously as others regarded religion. In 1861, the twenty-three-year-old student with a precisely trimmed mustache left Harvard in his junior year and enlisted in the 2nd Massachusetts Regiment, where he was commissioned a second lieutenant.

Shaw/54th Regiment Memorial

Over the next fifteen months, Shaw saw action in several bloody contests, including Ball's Bluff and Antietam, and rose to a post on the staff of his commander, Gen. John Gordon. Observing that the Union needed whatever help it could get, Shaw wrote a friend in July 1862 that the army ought to allow blacks to enlist and that "they would probably make a fine army after a little drill."

When the Emancipation Proclamation took effect on January 1, 1863, Massachusetts Governor John Andrew seized the moment to form the nation's first black regiment. He offered Shaw its command as a colonel; the young Brahmin first declined, then accepted.

Frederick Douglass may have promised African American volunteers "the same wages, the same rations, the same equipment, the same protection, the same treatment and the same bounty secured to white soldiers," but the U.S. Army had other ideas. At first, white privates were paid $13 per month, whereas black recruits of the same rank got only $7. The 54th Regiment refused to accept these discriminatory wages, and its soldiers went without pay until the Army granted them equal wages in 1864.

In their first weeks of action in July 1863, the soldiers of the 54th Regiment were kept busy as the Union prepared to take Charleston, South Carolina. They fought in several efforts to take strategic islands and helped rescue the 10th Connecticut Regiment from almost certain massacre. After a forty-eight-hour forced march, the regiment was then asked to lead the attack on Fort Wagner in Charleston Harbor. The order came in the form of a cordial invitation, but Shaw was quick to accept it. A battlefield veteran, he must have known the consequences.

As darkness fell on July 18, Shaw held his sword high and gave the order to charge. Union shells had battered Fort Wagner all day, but the rebels had not tired. When the 54th Regiment clambered up the parapets, they took the full force of Confederate fire. Shaw was among the first to fall; several hundred more would follow him. He and his dead comrades were later buried together in a mass grave.

The Confederates had meant to disgrace Robert Gould Shaw by so disposing of his corpse, but his family viewed the manner of his burial as an honor. When Union troops finally captured Fort Wagner in September, Francis George Shaw wrote to dissuade the army from any attempts to recover his son's body and separate it from those of his comrades-in-arms.

Sgt. William Carney, who rescued the regiment's fallen colors and returned to its lines despite four bullet wounds, became the first African American to receive the Congressional Medal of Honor.

60

1868

W. E. B. Du Bois is born in Great Barrington.

IN NEARLY A CENTURY ON THIS EARTH, WILLIAM Edward Burghardt Du Bois traveled from his birthplace in Great Barrington, Massachusetts, to his deathbed in Accra, Ghana. His arrival and departure—the one in America, the other in Africa—neatly symbolize the man's struggle with the two aspects of his self.

"One ever feels his twoness," wrote Du Bois in *The Souls of Black Folk*, a 1903 volume that plumbed the African American condition. "An American, a

Negro; two souls, two thoughts, two unreconciled strivings; two warring
ideals in one dark body, whose dogged strength alone keeps it from being torn
asunder."

In the busy mill town on the Housatonic, a young Du Bois felt the first
twinge of his dualism. Du Bois eventually abandoned the Berkshires
for Nashville, where in 1888 he graduated from Fisk University, a black
college.

Following a stay at the University of Berlin, Du Bois ventured home to
Massachusetts and Harvard University. He now devoted his life to the
study of history and the social sciences. His doctoral dissertation, *The
Suppression of the African Slave-Trade to the United States of America*, was
published in 1896. In it, Du Bois outlined clearly the role slavery had
played in the growth of the early American economy. Appointed a professor at Atlanta University, Du Bois began the first systematic examinations
of the conditions facing African Americans.

What Du Bois learned as he worked on his sociological investigations led
him to challenge the man who had come to represent—for white Americans, at least—the aspirations of all black Americans. A witness to the
effects of Jim Crow segregation laws, race riots, and lynchings, Du Bois
could not accept Booker T. Washington's policy of accommodation.
Instead, Du Bois called for elimination of all forms of racial segregation. In
1905 he and William Monroe Trotter, publisher of the African American
Boston Guardian, organized the militant "Niagara Movement" (named
for group's first meeting place in Niagara, Ontario), and in 1909, on the
centennial of Abraham Lincoln's birth, he and a group of socialists and
radicals, both black and white, founded the National Association for the
Advancement of Colored People.

In the years between the two world wars, Du Bois focused much of his
energy on ending white colonial rule in Africa. Gradually, his political
views drifted leftward, eventually leading him to support communism
and the Soviet Union. By the time of the cold war, a new generation of
NAACP leadership exiled Du Bois from its ranks. His plan to petition
the United Nations regarding human-rights violations against African
Americans in the United States was considered too militant. Among
those opposed to the Du Bois petition was NAACP board member
Eleanor Roosevelt.

During the Korean War, W. E. B. Du Bois, in his eighties, was tried for being an unregistered agent of a foreign power but was acquitted. Nevertheless, he was denied a U.S. passport for many years. When Du Bois finally could travel freely, he taunted American authorities by visiting China and the Soviet bloc. In 1961, the man who advocated Pan Africanism, an idea that all people of African background shared common concerns, moved to Ghana in West Africa and renounced his American citizenship. He died there in August 1963.

61

1868

Louisa May Alcott of Concord publishes Little Women.

LOUISA MAY ALCOTT AND HER FATHER, BRONSON Alcott, died two days apart in March 1888. They had shared the same birthday and were eulogized at the same funeral. A century later, they rest side by side in the earth and in the encyclopedia, as inextricably joined as they were in life.

The elder Alcott's esoteric intellectual musings as well as his impecuniousness exerted a great influence on Louisa May, the second of his four daughters born to his wife, Abigail May. In her early teens, Louisa conceived of herself both as a reformer and as responsible for her family's support. After stints as governess, seamstress, maid, teacher, and nurse, Louisa May Alcott turned at last to writing.

Raised in Concord among a community of radicals and intellectuals who included Emerson, Thoreau, and Fuller, Louisa witnessed the rise and fall of transcendentalism. Her father, who fancied himself an educational reformer, opened a series of children's schools in which the goal was not better test scores but to "awaken thought." At the Temple School in Boston, where Margaret Fuller briefly taught, children received an especially gentle form of instruction. Punishment for classroom misbehavior consisted of the children hitting the teacher with a ruler.

In 1839 Bronson reluctantly closed the Temple School, and following a trip to England, he and British philosopher Charles Lane organized what they called "a new Eden" on a hillside in Harvard, Massachusetts. Residents of "Fruitlands," which opened in 1843, were committed to being vegetarians and refused to wear wool (shearing deprived the sheep of its natural covering) or cotton (which was produced by slave labor). They even attempted to haul plows themselves (rather than burden horses with the work). The experiment—impractical even by typical utopian standards—failed within a few months.

The zeal for reform that characterized the lives of Bronson and Abigail May Alcott was taken up by their daughter, but in more moderate fashion. Louisa served as a volunteer nurse in the Civil War, an experience that formed the basis of the well-received *Hospital Sketches* (1863). Throughout her life, she signed letters, "Yours for reform of all kinds."

Louisa wrote many novels and short stories, including dozens of potboilers (some of these under a pseudonym, A. M. Barnard). No less a critic than Henry James remarked of *Moods*, an early Alcott novel from 1864, "The two most striking facts with regard to [the book] are the author's ignorance of human nature and her self-confidence in spite of this ignorance."

When Louisa accepted a commission from a Boston publisher to write "a girls' story," the self-confidence remained, though she hardly proved ignorant of the human nature of girls and women. She knew her sisters, after all, and her mother. Most important, she was keenly aware of the forces working against her female characters as they sought fulfillment and happiness in a world that severely restricted their choices.

Immediately on publication in 1868, *Little Women* (Part I) was a critical and commercial hit, establishing Meg, Jo, Beth, and Amy firmly in the hearts of American girls. (Part II followed a year later.) Spurred by this success, Louisa eventually completed a full chronicle of the lives of the March family sisters as they progress to womanhood in *Little Men* (1871) and *Jo's Boys* (1886).

62

Fire sweeps through downtown Boston.

THE FIRST ALARM RANG FROM BOX 52, ON THE corner of Lincoln and Bedford streets, at 7:24 P.M. on November 9, 1872. A general alarm sounded barely fifteen minutes later. The Great Boston Fire of 1872 burned out of control until the following afternoon.

From the first flickers in a five-story granite block at Kingston and Summer streets, the fire eventually destroyed 776 buildings with a total assessed value of $13.5 million and contents valued at $60 million. Flames killed thirty-three people and devoured a sixty-five-acre area bounded by Washington Street on the west, Summer Street on the south, Liberty Square on the east, and State Street on the north.

The fire gutted many buildings surviving from Boston's colonial era. It leveled with equal force the offices of the *Transcript*, the preferred journal of Boston's Brahmins, and those of the *Pilot*, a Catholic weekly then edited by John Boyle O'Reilly. Miraculously spared was the Old South Meeting House at Milk and Washington streets. From its clock tower down Milk Street to the harbor, the city was transformed into a wasteland.

Long before the fire, the downtown district had already lost its fashionable status as a residential quarter for Boston's wealthier merchants. Shops and businesses gradually replaced homes throughout the mid-century. On delicately curved Franklin Street, Charles Bulfinch's elegant Tontine Crescent, a block of handsome townhouses, was razed in 1858 to make way for undistinguished offices.

Residences that were still standing ignited like tinder in the great fire's path. Many of the homes—housing for the Irish and other immigrants who worked on the nearby waterfront's bustling docks—were in poor condition, making them particularly hazardous.

In the early stages of the battle, firefighters became frustrated when outdated water pipes delivered insufficient pressure through their hoses.

Old South Meeting House

Contributing to the fire's magnitude was an epidemic of distemper among the department's horses. Men had to haul the steam-driven pumps and other heavy equipment.

At the Western Union office on State Street, telegraph operators pleaded for help from every fire department within fifty miles of Boston. Altogether, 2,163 firefighters from thirty-one neighboring cities and towns answered the call. Of the thirty-three people who perished in the blaze, thirteen were firefighters.

The nearly spontaneous rebirth of downtown Boston became a testament to the prudence of well-insured property owners. In the decade following the Great Fire of 1872, the city's center filled with buildings of flame-resistant stone and iron.

1874

Harvard and McGill face off in "Boston football."

A BASIC YET RADICAL INNOVATION DISTINGUISHED "Boston football" from the other types of American football played elsewhere in the eastern United States, mostly at elite universities. In essence, this was the same distinction that had earlier separated rugby from soccer: rather than simply kick a round leather ball to move it forward on the field and score a goal, players in the "Boston game" were allowed to throw the ball and, later, to run with it.

College football traditionally celebrates its birthday as November 6, 1869. On that fall day, teams from Rutgers and Princeton squared off on a vacant grass lot in New Brunswick, New Jersey. (Rutgers won, 6–4.) The football they played, however, was nothing like contemporary American football. Teams fielded twenty-five players to a side; no running or throwing was permitted; the ball was advanced by foot, head, or shoulder. Players scored by kicking a round ball through an opponent's goal, which was 8 yards wide on a field 120 yards long and 75 yards wide.

The "Boston game" had evolved from a rough-and-tumble sport played on Boston Common from before the Civil War. In 1863 the Oneida Football Club was formed by students from English, Latin, and other city high schools as the first organized football club in the United States. Not surprisingly, prominent family names figured on the Oneida roster, including Lawrence, Peabody, and Bowditch.

In three years of play, Oneida never lost a game or permitted an opponent to score. As the "Boston game" was then played, however, scoring a goal amounted to the same thing as winning (thus all games ended as 1–0). In Oneida football, there was no letup except when the ball went out of bounds. The round ball could be tossed as well as kicked.

Presumably, Oneida's blue-blooded players graduated from high school and carried their football rules with them to Harvard. When a group of colleges including Yale, Columbia, Rutgers, and Princeton gathered in New

York City in October 1873, they sought to establish a uniform set of football rules. Harvard was invited to join them, but declined. The Crimson did not want to give up the Boston version of the game.

On May 14 and 15, 1874, a football team from Montreal's McGill University visited Cambridge for a two-game series with Harvard. McGill's game strongly emphasized running and tackling and was even more like rugby than the Boston game. Harvard football rules permitted throwing and even dribbling the ball, but the game remained like soccer in its heavy reliance on kicking.

Harvard won the first game, 3–0; the second game was a scoreless tie. The Crimson boys were nevertheless impressed with the game McGill played, and they quickly adopted the Montreal style of running with the ball and tackling opponents. Harvard's first football game against an American team came in 1875, when the team played Tufts University twice, once in the spring and again in the fall. On November 13, 1875, Harvard played its first football game against Yale, establishing a legendary rivalry.

Later that month, Harvard, Yale, Princeton, and Columbia gathered in Springfield to form the Intercollegiate Football Association. The rules they adopted were Harvard's. Within five years, the "Boston game," as revised, became the dominant form of football played in America.

64

1875

Mary Baker Eddy founds Christian Science.

LIVING ALONE IN SWAMPSCOTT, MARY BAKER FELT hopeless. She had endured various maladies in her life and, for a time at least, a charismatic spiritual healer had helped to cure her condition. The healer, Phineas Quimby, died in 1866, and Baker's illness—a kind of spinal ailment—returned shortly afterward. An accident, apparently a fall on ice, compounded the pain.

Mary Baker Eddy Home, Swampscott

Baker, forty-five, turned to the Bible for solace. In the New Testament she read an account of healing by Jesus. She was cured. The experience led her to believe that all disease was a product of the mind.

In *Science and Health*, which Baker published in 1875 and which appeared in 382 revised editions throughout the rest of her life, Baker outlined her new philosophy. "Christian Science," as she called it, sought to restore "primitive Christianity and its lost element of healing."

Christian Science urged followers to throw off the limitations of flesh by accepting "the mind of Christ." Prayer, which some considered necessary for spiritual redemption in the next world, acquired curative powers in this one. Christian Science required men and women to look beyond material appearances to find the true spiritual order.

The Church of Christ, Scientist was formally established in Boston in 1879; later, the church was reorganized as the First Church of Christ, Scientist. The Mother Church in Boston, which opened in 1894, was made responsible for the various branches around the world. The Christian Science Publishing Society began publishing *The Christian Science Monitor* newspaper in 1908.

Mary Baker married one of her followers, Asa Gilbert Eddy, in 1877. Her third husband, Eddy died in 1882, and Baker ended her long life enduring alone the pain that had plagued her since childhood. She became something of a recluse and feared what she called "malicious animal magnetism" directed at her by Christian Science's detractors. Baker died in Chestnut Hill of pneumonia at eighty-nine.

65

1876

Alexander Graham Bell, working in a Boston garret, invents the telephone.

ON MARCH 3, 1876, THE APPLICANT'S TWENTY-NINTH birthday, the U.S. Patent Office in Washington granted Patent No. 174,465 for "the method of, and apparatus for, transmitting vocal or other sounds telegraphically . . . by causing electrical undulations, similar in form to the vibrations of the air accompanying the said vocal or other sounds."

At least that was the principle. Alexander Graham Bell, a man overworked to the point of confusion, had not demonstrated that any such improvement in the telegraph would actually transmit human conversation. For nearly a year, he and his assistant Thomas Watson had only transmitted recognizable vocal sounds—shouts, mostly, and those were heard but faintly at the receiving end. Their device could not yet carry a single intelligible sentence from one room of a Boston garret to another.

The Scots-born inventor first came to the commonwealth in 1871 on a lecture tour demonstrating his father's system for teaching the hearing-impaired to speak. "Visible Speech for the Deaf" was essentially a written code indicating how one should position the lips, tongue, and palate to make the usual sounds of speech. His success with the program soon led Bell to open his own school for the deaf. In 1873 he was appointed a distinguished professor of "vocal physiology" at Boston University.

All the while, A. Graham Bell (as he preferred to be known) worked nights seeking to perfect what he called a "harmonic telegraph" capable of transmitting sound rather than merely dots and dashes. He was convinced the idea could lead to sending human conversation over wire, but he lacked the mechanical and electrical expertise to realize his dream.

In the shop where he sometimes brought his devices for repairs, Bell found Thomas Watson. The self-taught electrician seemed capable of translating the professor's vision and enthusiasm into reality. At an improvised laboratory on Court Street, the pair struggled to perfect the harmonic telegraph, which transmitted its first sounds in June 1875. When success appeared near, a secretive Bell chose to move the lab, himself, and Watson to a nearby boardinghouse. For a rent of $4 a week, they conducted experiments in one attic room and slept in the other.

March 10, 1876, saw Watson experimenting with raising the volume of transmitted vocal sounds. He rigged a wire from a cup of sulfuric acid to generate an electrical current (much like a typical battery circuit). Watson connected one end of the device and left Bell to go to the other room for a test. As he later recorded in a memoir, Watson next bent to the receiver and was surprised to hear Bell exclaim, "Mr. Watson, come here, I want you!" The clumsy professor had spilled dangerous sulfuric acid on his clothes. "The tone of his voice indicated he needed help," his assistant remembered.

On October 9, Bell and Watson gave a demonstration of the invention to a group of Boston journalists. They carried on what is recorded as the first "long-distance" telephone conversation—from the downtown laboratory to the Walworth Manufacturing Company offices in Cambridgeport, two miles away, using a borrowed telegraph line.

In May 1877, the first telephone for business use on a private line was installed from the State Street offices of Stone & Downer, bankers, to the home of its president, Roswell C. Downer, on Central Street, Somerville. That month there were six telephones in commercial use in Greater Boston. By November the number had jumped to three thousand, and in 1878 the first telephone directory was published in Boston.

66

The New England Society for the Suppression of Vice is established in Boston.

WHEN THE NEW ENGLAND SOCIETY FOR THE
Suppression of Vice was established on May 28, 1878,
it joined the august company of other such groups
in London, New York, Philadelphia, Chicago, and
Cincinnati. Their mutual goal was the "suppression
of all agencies tending to corrupt the morals of youth." Characteristically
for the descendants of Puritan witch-hunters, only the Boston group
achieved a kind of sublime level of moral fussiness.

Keeping the Puritans pure, to paraphrase H. L. Mencken's words in the
American Mercury, required more than the ordinary censor's diligence. In
one notable year, volunteer members of the captious New England Watch
and Ward Society (adopted in 1891, the name referred to Boston's original
police force) reviewed a weighty reading list of novels by H. G. Wells,
Sinclair Lewis, Ernest Hemingway, Sherwood Anderson, and John Dos
Passos. All were properly examined and subsequently "banned in Boston."
Typical charges were that a work was "pernicious," "filthy," or "Frenchy."

Among book publishers, "banned in Boston" became an eagerly sought mark
of disgrace. Those three words all but guaranteed them a bestseller. Indeed,
unscrupulous editors were guilty of intentionally selecting to publish volumes
of obviously "immoral literature" in order to attract the society's proscription.
Booksellers, too, collected banned books together for their sales appeal.

In late Victorian America, urban crime was rampant, and city police forces
were hostage to corruption and political influence. Much to their credit, volunteer watchdog groups of the period were able to force a reluctant government to perform its neglected duties and to enforce the law. Rigged lotteries
and suspicious gambling halls were shut down, and notorious prostitution rings
were broken as the direct result of efforts by genuinely concerned citizens.

Emboldened by early successes, however, Brahmins went further than petty crime in their vendetta against "evils that require correction." Boston storekeepers were accordingly cited for displaying "immodest advertising" in their shop windows; all manner of immoral literature was forbidden to be sold; and allegedly obscene motion pictures were heavily edited. William Makepeace Thackeray's *Catherine,* in one instance of fairly typical Puritan zealousness, was put down by a well-placed Watch and Ward Society critic as a "horrid story of a lot of criminals."

In 1925 Clarence Darrow, the usually brilliant defense lawyer, met his match in the New England Watch and Ward Society. The attorney's pleas on behalf of Theodore Dreiser's masterpiece *An American Tragedy* fell on the deaf ears of a Massachusetts Supreme Court justice, and the book's New York publisher was duly convicted on obscenity charges.

At the society's Boston offices, shelves sagged with pernicious books, and files bulged with Frenchy photographs, all of which could be reviewed only by paid-up board members. Private exhibitions were given of film scenes recovered from the censor's cutting room floor. Puritanism, in Mencken's definition, may be "the haunting fear that someone, somewhere, may be happy," yet membership in the New England Watch and Ward Society had its moments. In the 1950s, the group attacked illicit gambling rather than obscene literature. In 1967, it was renamed the New England Citizens Crime Commission.

67

1881

Frederick Law Olmsted begins work on the "Emerald Necklace."

THE IMPULSE IS TO CALL THEM BOSTON'S CROWN jewels. The arrangement of parks and ponds that make up the "Emerald Necklace" certainly merit high tribute, yet the city wears its green and open spaces as casually and comfortably as if they were only costume jewelry.

Stretching for five miles from the urban confines of Boston Common to the open country of Franklin Park, the Emerald Necklace takes in an astounding variety of landscapes. Thickets and open glades; brackish marshes and freshwater ponds; wild forests and manicured flower beds—these and other elements unfold along the system's route like a nineteenth-century novel dense with subplots and richly populated with idiosyncratic characters.

Frederick Law Olmsted suffered from poor eyesight as a young man, yet he trained himself to be a thorough and thoughtful observer. As a reporter for *The New York Times* from 1853 to 1855, the pro-abolitionist Olmsted sent weekly dispatches from the South detailing the degrading character of slavery. He also wrote several incisive travelogues, including *Walks and Talks of an American Farmer in England* (1850) and *A Journey Through Texas* (1857).

In 1857 Olmsted became the first superintendent of New York City's Central Park. He was thirty-five, and in a peripatetic youth he had acquired wide experience. He had served as a seaman in the China trade and as a farmer in his native Connecticut; he had variously studied engineering, science, and agriculture; and he had endured financial failure in business. Whether these amount to ideal qualifications for a landscape architect is debatable, but Olmsted was perhaps as well prepared as anyone in pre–Civil War America to imagine a new form for the wasteland at what were then New York City's northern limits. A year later, he and collaborator Calvert Vaux won an open design competition for Central Park with a plan they called "Greensward."

From Yosemite Park to the U.S. Capitol grounds, Frederick Law Olmsted imposed over the next half century a wholly personal vision for landscape design and the preservation of open space. His six principles of landscape design included scenery, suitability, sanitation, subordination, separation, and spaciousness.

Above all, Olmsted had a powerful faith in the ability of landscape architecture to promote a sense of community and to have a positive impact on society. He was deeply aware that the development of public parks in America—once a place of boundless open spaces—coincided with an unprecedented growth of the nation's cities. "Is it not reasonable to regard it as a self-preserving instinct of civilization?" he asked pointedly in 1881.

That same year, while on a winter visit to Henry Hobson Richardson's Brookline estate, Olmsted woke to behold a snow-blanketed suburban landscape and a snowplow clearing the street. "This is a civilized community," he reportedly told the architect of Trinity Church. "I'm going to live here." In 1883 Olmsted moved his family and business practice from New York to a renovated farmhouse at the corner of Dudley and Warren streets.

Olmsted had already begun work in 1878 to create a Back Bay park for the area known as the Fens, a swamp at the confluence of the Muddy River, Stony Creek, and the Charles River. Gradually his plan for the Fens grew into a revolutionary treatment for a continuous city park system. The design scheme for what we know today as the Emerald Necklace was first presented to the Boston Parks Commission in 1881. Of one prominent jewel in the necklace, Jamaica Pond, Olmsted wrote seductively that it should be "for the most part shaded by a fine natural forest growth to be brought out overhangingly, darkening the water's edge and favoring great beauty in reflections and flickering half-lights."

The effect today is as the author imagined more than a century ago.

68

1886

Emily Dickinson dies at the family home in Amherst.

SOME COMBINATION OF CONDITIONS AND EVENTS IN her early life, which we may never entirely understand, drove Emily Dickinson of Amherst to spin a lush cocoon of silken words to shield herself from the world. Unhappily, the butterfly she became never emerged while she was alive.

Today, the remarkable volume of poetry Dickinson composed is judged among the best written in English in the nineteenth century.

Dickinson home, Amherst

The vindicating judgment of history would likely have surprised Dickinson's own contemporaries. To a close friend, she was a "partially cracked poetess." The unkind remark had some basis in her strange habits. For many years, Dickinson dressed only in white, like a nun in a habit. She scrupulously avoided visitors, and for the last twenty years of her life she did not even set her foot outside the family property in Amherst, Massachusetts. Upon her death, her coffin was carried from the family home through neighboring backyards to the cemetery in order to avoid undue public notice.

In her correspondence and whatever poetry she shared with friends and family, Dickinson trimmed her language so severely that she often baffled her readers. Beside the voluminous spreading oak of typical Victorian verse and prose, her intentionally diminished work appears like a bonsai tree.

Emily Dickinson was born December 10, 1830, at a time when Amherst was nearly a frontier village. She attended Mount Holyoke Female Seminary (now College), but left after the first year, apparently because of homesickness. While her father, Edward, served a term in Congress in 1855, Emily traveled once to Washington with her sister; it was the longest time Emily ever spent away from home.

On the return leg of that trip, Dickinson heard Rev. Charles Wadsworth preach in Philadelphia. The darkly attractive minister became her mentor and "dearest earthly friend" and even visited her in Amherst in 1860. His departure for a church in California in 1862 precipitated the first of Dickinson's several bouts with serious depression.

The great love of Dickinson's life was undoubtedly her father. Edward Dickinson was a puritanical figure—"he steps like Cromwell," his daughter wrote. Through her father, Emily Dickinson acquired a Puritan's character-istic fascination with death and the fate of the soul. With her deep love of nature, quick wit, and skeptical eye, Emily Dickinson transformed this morbid obsession into literature.

Dickinson wrote nearly eighteen hundred poems, but she published only seven during her lifetime, five of those in the *Springfield Republican*. Her surviving sister, Lavinia, published the first collection in 1890. Not until 1955 did all her poems finally appear in print.

69

1891

James Naismith invents the game of basketball, in Springfield.

THE NEW GAME MIGHT HAVE BEEN CALLED "boxball." Sometime in mid-December 1891, James Naismith asked a janitor at what is today Springfield College to find a pair of fifteen-by-fifteen-inch boxes. The custodian instead returned with two half-bushel peach baskets, which Naismith ordered to be tied to the balcony railing at either end of the school gym.

A physical education instructor for the International Young Men's Chris-tian Association (YMCA) Training School, Naismith called his class into the chilly gymnasium. The eighteen young men who were gathered saw the janitor and a companion seated atop ladders arranged beside the hang-ing peach baskets. "Hunh!" Frank Mahan, one of the students, muttered derisively. "Another new game!"

Basketball Hall of Fame, Springfield

Spurred by a school dean who wanted his students to continue their athletic training indoors after the football season ended, James Naismith had experimented before with "new games." For this latest trial, Naismith drew liberally from lacrosse, soccer, and other existing sports. Lacrosse suggested the original positions of his players, for example, and a soccer ball was used because it was soft and too large to be concealed. Players were not allowed to run with the ball, which had to be tossed from one to another and into a goal. Holding, pushing, and tripping were barred. Naismith aimed to create a noncontact indoor sport that provided exercise for the whole body and required sharp mental attention.

Incredibly, the hybrid game was an instant success. Naismith published his list of simple rules in the school's campus newspaper on January 15, 1892, and local athletic associations were soon clamoring for copies. By year's end, the new game had even taken on an international dimension, when it was played for the first time in Mexico and Canada. Basketball soon spread overseas to France, China, Australia, and India.

Setting aside his initial skepticism, Frank Mahan became a devotee of "the new game." In fact, Mahan gets credit as the first person to call the sport "basket ball" (which at first was written as two words). "We have a basket and a ball," Mahan irrefutably observed, "so 'basket ball' would seem a good name for it."

The "basket" evolved quickly and the game along with it. Cylindrical baskets of heavy woven wire replaced peach baskets almost immediately. In 1893 these were replaced in their turn by "baskets" with iron rims and braided cord netting manufactured in Providence at the Narragansett Machine Company. Nevertheless, basket nets were not opened at the bottom until 1912. The first true "basket balls," made by the Overman Wheel Company of Chicopee Falls, replaced soccer balls in 1894, the same year the free throw was introduced.

The first recorded women's basketball game was played barely four months after the first men's game. The teams were mostly drawn from women working in the Springfield Y's stenographers' pool, among them Maude Sherman, who later became Mrs. Naismith. On March 22, 1893, Senda Berenson Abbott introduced basket ball to the women students of Smith College in Northampton. Male spectators were not allowed to watch the bloomer-clad players.

A century after its invention, according to curators at the Naismith Memorial Basketball Hall of Fame in Springfield, basketball has conquered the world. The first two sides of nine players each (reduced to five players in 1895) have multiplied to some 18 million professionals and amateurs who dribble, fake, and shoot their way around neighborhood courts and in enormous indoor arenas.

70

1892

Lizzie Borden takes an ax. . . .

FALL RIVER LEGEND, A 1948 BALLET BY AGNES DE Mille with a score by Morton Gould; Lizzie Borden, a 1965 opera by Jack Beeson; and a 1934 play, Nine Pine Street, starring Lillian Gish, are among the list of ambitious works of art that all share for their inspiration the same famous crime. None of them, however, is likely to replace in the public mind four lines of cheap doggerel, composer unknown.

Lizzie Borden took an ax
and gave her mother forty whacks.
And when she saw what she had done,
she gave her father forty-one.

In all accounts of the Borden murders, Lizzie is guilty and, frequently, she has done the deed for love. Most important to her, however, if not to either artists or posterity, is that Lizzie Borden was swiftly judged "not guilty" by a jury after only ninety minutes' deliberation. Those who had followed the case closely roundly seconded that finding.

No less an institution than *The New York Times* made its opinion of the Fall River court proceedings perfectly plain: "The acquittal of this most unfortunate and cruelly persecuted woman was, by its promptness, in effect, a condemnation of the police authorities of Fall River and of the legal officers who secured the indictment and have conducted the trial," declared an editorial. "It was a declaration, not only that the prisoner was guiltless, but there was never any reason to suppose that she was guilty."

Indeed, Fall River was named as the guilty party in place of Borden. It deserved conviction (in the New York press, at least) for being a slovenly and provincial backwater. "The town is not a large one," the *Times* editorial pointed out bluntly. "The police is of the usual inept and stupid and muddleheaded sort that such towns manage to get for themselves."

Pity the muddleheaded police, though. The scene they found at 62 Second Street the afternoon of August 4, 1892, would have muddled anyone's thinking. According to a contemporary account, Andrew Borden, sixty-nine, lay lifeless on the living room sofa. The president of the Union Savings Bank was a stern-faced Yankee capitalist who had accumulated a large fortune through real estate and other investments. Borden died from a deep wound to the left temple, possibly by the blow of an ax. His left eye was dug out, and a cut extended the length of his nose. Upstairs, Mrs. Borden, sixty-three and the banker's second wife, lay in a pool of her own blood. She had been similarly attacked. "Hacked to pieces" was how one newspaper headline described her condition. Otherwise, nothing seemed to have been stolen, and the house was not ransacked.

Suspicion fell immediately on someone the papers called "a sturdy Portuguese," a laborer who worked on a farm Borden owned and who had visited his employer earlier in the day to demand wages owed him. Several arrests of suspicious persons were made—one Portuguese man was taken into custody as well as two Russian Jews. "They were locked up simply by way of precaution," noted a report in the *Boston Advertiser*.

The theory quickly took root among the Fall River press and public that the Borden murders were committed by someone who lived in the house— either Lizzie J. Borden, Andrew Borden's thirty-two-year-old daughter from his first marriage, or possibly the family maid, Bridget Sullivan.

On August 11, police abruptly arrested Lizzie. Evidence and motive were scant. No ax or murder weapon of any kind was ever found. The state would suggest in court that Lizzie Borden was jealous of her stepmother and was afraid she would not receive a fair share of her father's estate when he died, but the charge was never substantiated.

Because Lizzie Borden said nothing, because she did not cry or show much of any emotion throughout her long ordeal, the prosecution felt that was proof enough of her guilt. The jury decided that it was not.

Lizzie Borden died in 1927, friendless and alone. In her will, the largest single bequest was for $30,000 to the local chapter of the Animal Rescue League.

71

1893

In Springfield, Frank Duryea test-drives the first American gasoline-powered automobile.

AT THE CLOSE OF THE NINETEENTH CENTURY, numerous inventors and entrepreneurs across Europe and America contributed to the perfection of the internal combustion engine, the key element in the automobile as we know it today.

Jean Joseph Etienne Lenoir, a Belgian working in Paris, patented an internal combustion engine that burned coal gas in 1860. Improvements in petroleum products steered others to use more volatile and more practical gasoline for engine fuel. In 1885 Karl Benz put a one-cylinder, gasoline-powered engine on a three-wheeled vehicle with a steel frame—essentially a motor-tricycle. He sold his first four-wheeled Benz automobile two years later. In 1886 Gottlieb Daimler and Wilhelm Maybach mounted their own high-speed internal combustion engine on a modified carriage chassis. Daimler Motoren-Gesellschaft opened for commercial automobile production in 1890.

Americans showed a keen interest in the many improvements made to self-propelled vehicles, but especially those powered by steam and electricity. They were relatively late in latching onto the gasoline-powered, internal combustion engine as the technology of choice.

Massachusetts inventors were no different from compatriots in other states. Beginning in 1859, Sylvester Roper of Roxbury produced a series of steam-powered coaches, including a two-passenger four-wheeler built in 1863. In 1888 Philip W. Pratt built the nation's first electric carriage and operated a manufacturing plant in Boston's South End. In Brookline, German émigré Charles Holtzer assembled an electric car in 1892 for a wealthy Bostonian from parts purchased in Europe. The driver was involved in what was probably the state's first automobile accident, also in Brookline, in June 1893.

Gradually, mechanics and inventors in Massachusetts and around the country became frustrated with the limitations on speed and efficiency posed by heavy batteries and steam engines. Internal combustion engines were smaller, lighter, and more powerful. The Americans copied diagrams of German designs published in *Scientific American* and made their own modifications.

Among those fascinated by what the Germans had accomplished were Frank and Charles Duryea, Illinois-born brothers who worked in a bicycle factory at Chicopee. Beginning in 1891, Charles Duryea prepared designs for a one-cylinder, two-cycle engine to be installed on a horse carriage.

When an investor agreed to stake the pair $1,000, the Duryeas rented space at a Springfield machine shop. Frank Duryea, the more mechanically inclined of the brothers, began the car's construction in the summer of

1892, and Charles soon returned to Peoria, Illinois. Notwithstanding a bout with typhoid fever that interrupted his labors, Frank Duryea persevered for the next year.

On September 21, 1893, Frank Duryea finally tested his automobile on the road. The noisy car, hampered by a transmission problem, traveled only two hundred feet before stalling. By January 18, 1894, however, Frank Duryea drove six miles round-trip from his shop to his investor's home at a top speed of eight miles per hour.

Eventually reunited, the Duryea brothers formed the Duryea Motor Wagon Company, the nation's first gasoline automobile manufacturer, in 1895. On Thanksgiving Day that year, they won America's first automobile race, from Chicago to Evanston, Illinois, and back. The Duryea car averaged slightly over five miles per hour, but it had beaten three Benz automobiles as well as several American-made electric cars. The Duryeas' company folded in 1898 when Frank and Charles argued over division of its ownership.

The most memorable contribution to automobile history from Massachusetts was the Stanley Steamer. The Stanley twins, Francis Edgar and Freelan Oscar, began producing steam-powered automobiles in Newton in 1897. At an 1898 automobile show in Cambridge, a Stanley Steamer set a world speed record (36 miles per hour). The Stanley Motor Carriage Company closed in 1923.

72

1897

John McDermott wins the first Boston Marathon.

AT THE FIRST MODERN OLYMPICS, HELD IN ATHENS in 1896, the American field and track squad were all members of the Boston Athletic Association. Founded in 1887, the BAA attracted to its ranks the vigorous sons of Boston's merchant princes. These athletes had competed as college students, and they wanted to maintain their fit conditions even as gentlemen.

Devoted amateurs, the early BAA members disdained those who were paid money or ran in races where betting was allowed. It has been pointed out that this cult of amateurism, though admirable, was one that only wealthy men such as Boston Brahmins could afford to abide by. Indeed, amateurism likely became a convenient instrument to keep out of sports "the wrong kind of people"—professionals who usually were drawn from among the working class, particularly immigrants.

The marathon derived from the ancient Greek practice of employing fleet-footed messengers to carry important communications from one city to another. In a legend with a historical basis, Pheidippides in 490 BCE covered twenty-four miles from the battle on the Plains of Marathon to Athens to bring word of the Persians' defeat. "Rejoice, we conquer!" Pheidippides supposedly declared on his arrival—before he collapsed dead.

In 1896, the revival of the Olympics caught the public's attention with the decision to include a twenty-four-mile marathonlike race. The unprecedented running contest promised a romantic spectacle with an appealing hint of danger. Appropriately, a Greek won the race in two hours, fifty-five minutes, and twenty seconds.

On Patriot's Day, April 19, 1897, eighteen men gathered at the starting line in Ashland for the first Boston Marathon, sponsored by the BAA. Six runners represented several New York athletic clubs, including John J. McDermott, a lithographer, who had won the only other U.S. marathon yet held (from Stamford, Connecticut, to New York City in 1896). The Boston favorite, Dick Grant, was a Harvard man and a BAA member.

Ten runners finished the course, with the last arriving at the BAA clubhouse on Boylston Street four hours and ten minutes after the starting gun was fired. The winner was John McDermott, who fought cramps and blisters to cross the finish line at two hours, fifty-five minutes, and ten seconds—ten seconds ahead of the Olympic winner's time, and a new world record. Newspaper accounts estimated that twenty-five thousand spectators lined the marathon route, which was rather informally guarded. In the last few hundred yards of the race, McDermott weaved through a funeral procession moving somberly down Massachusetts Avenue.

A Bostonian did not win the Boston Marathon until 1916, when Arthur Ross crossed the finish line ahead of the pack.

73

1897

The first subway in America opens at Park Street Under.

AT THE END OF THE NINETEENTH CENTURY, BOSTON'S tremendously popular system of interconnecting electric trolley lines converged downtown along Tremont Street near Boston Common and the Old Granary Burying Ground. Streetcars gathered toward the center of the city's bustling business and retail district like metal filings around a powerful magnet.

Eventually even City Hall and the state legislature on nearby Beacon Hill conceded that Boston had a transit problem. Surveys were ordered and proposals evaluated. In the meantime, streetcar blockades worsened, and pedestrians despaired of ever crossing safely from Boston Common to their favorite shops on Winter Street.

Many corrective schemes were considered. One proposal suggested clearing a path for a twenty-five-foot-wide transit "alley" between Washington and Tremont streets. Another advocated widening Tremont Street to improve the flow of trolley cars or else erecting an elevated railway bridge high above the pavement. A variety of plans offered streetcar access to Boston Common either on the surface or along trenches.

At the same time, travelers who visited London, Paris, and Budapest returned with praises for those cities' revolutionary new underground trolley lines. Arguments were made in favor of such "subways" and were recorded in the Boston Transit Commission's first annual report.

"The subway destroys but little property," the commission noted. "The subway eliminates the danger which pedestrians now encounter in crossing tracks; the subway increases traffic capacity by removing from the surface one important class of traffic; the subway relieves the streets of the posts and network of wires necessary in the overhead trolley system; [and] the subway relieves the street of the noise of the streetcar, the rumble and jar of the wheels, the hum of the motor and the clang of the bell."

Bostonians of the Victorian Age had apparently no reason to be nostalgic for the trolley's ding-ding-ding and clang-clang-clang. They were happy enough, indeed, to find an excuse to put it out of sight, at least along crowded Tremont Street, and they were willing to pay for it. In 1893 and 1894 the state legislature voted to fund a $5 million subway system, and construction work began at Boston Common on March 28, 1895.

On schedule and under budget, the nation's first subway line finally opened on September 1, 1897. The cars ran only the length of the Common, from Park Street to Boylston Street, at first. By month's end, however, stations at Scollay Square and elsewhere were opened, connecting "Park Street Under" to cars running on the West End Railway Company and the Boston Elevated Railway Company. Eventually a two-mile subway system stretched from Back Bay to North Station.

74 | 1903

The Boston Pilgrims face the Pittsburgh Pirates in the first World Series.

IN 1900, BAN JOHNSON, A FORMER CINCINNATI sportswriter, set in motion changes that forever altered the character of baseball. As president of what was formerly known as the Western League, Johnson announced that new baseball franchises were set to open the following season in Boston, Philadelphia, Baltimore, and Washington. The Western League—with teams in Cleveland and Chicago, among other midwestern cities—was renamed the American League.

Johnson had the gall to declare that the American League was to be considered a "major" league on a par with the well-established National League. To ensure that no one questioned its "major league" status, Johnson announced that American League owners would not honor the National League's $2,400 salary cap.

Not surprisingly, 111 of the 182 players for the American League's first season were attracted from the lower-paying National League. Triple Crown winner Nap Lajoie, for example, moved across town from the Philadelphia Phillies to the upstart Philadelphia Athletics. Pitcher Cy Young also bolted to the American League team in Boston. By 1903 a truce was reached between the two baseball leagues that ended American League raids on National League teams. Bleacher and standing-room tickets sold that season for fifty cents, while grandstand seats were a buck.

The more peaceful environment begged for an interleague championship contest. The National League pennant winners, the Pittsburgh Pirates, now challenged the American League leaders, the Boston Pilgrims (ancestors of the present-day Red Sox), to a "World Series." A nine-game series was arranged, with the first three and last two games to be played in Boston and the middle four in Pittsburgh.

The idea of a World Series wasn't entirely new. Twenty-one years before, when the term was first coined, the National League champion Chicago team first experimented with such a contest against the American Association champs from Cincinnati. The play in these early World Series was erratic, even farcical. The 1885 matchup saw 101 errors in seven games (27 errors were made in the final seventh game). That year's series ended in a draw, with three wins and a tie each for the St. Louis Browns and the Chicago White Stockings.

In the first game of the 1903 World Series (officially recorded as the first such matchup), Boston's Cy Young, a twenty-eight-game winner in the regular season, was walloped for four runs in the first inning. The Pilgrims eventually lost, 7–3. When the Pilgrims and Pirates returned to Boston for an eighth game, the American League champs held a one-game lead over their National League rivals. A ninth game proved unnecessary, however, as pitcher Bill Dinneen won his third game of the series by a score of 3–0.

A strike threat by the Boston Pilgrims nearly prevented the first World Series. The players' contracts expired on September 30, and the series was to be played well into October. Team owner Henry Killilea was told he must pay his men two weeks' additional wages as well the entire club's share of the series' gate. Killilea agreed to the extra pay but successfully held out for a club owner's share of ticket sales. To boost the take, he charged admission to every attending sportswriter and even the owner of the Pittsburgh Pirates.

75

1912

The "Bread and Roses" strike hits Lawrence's textile mills.

WITH NEW YEAR'S DAY 1912, MASSACHUSETTS PUT into force a set of labor laws that sent a tidal wave of reform over American industry. The regulations set maximum working hours for women and children at fifty-four hours weekly. In addition, a new law required a minimum wage to be paid female employees that will "supply the necessary cost of living and maintain the worker in health."

For their time, these were progressive, even revolutionary laws. Massachusetts frequently led the nation in labor reform, though the standards first introduced seem ludicrous today. In 1842, for example, the legislature restricted the working day for children to ten hours.

For factory workers, January 11 was to be the first payday under the new laws. In Lawrence, nearly forty thousand toiling workers gravely feared that textile mill owners would use a shortened working week as an excuse to cut wages. Envelopes were distributed, then hurriedly opened. The

Former textile mill, Lawrence

workers' worst fears were realized: on average, each paycheck was short about thirty-two cents. Among those who typically earned just over eight dollars per week, the pay cut was substantial.

Inside the mills, angry words were spoken in Polish, Italian, French, and other tongues. The mostly unorganized workers left their looms in a spontaneous strike, first at the Everett Mills and later at the American Woolen Company.

As a congressional investigation later showed, conditions in Lawrence were so abominable that the mills were like tinderboxes waiting for a spark. Husbands and wives—and most children over the age of fourteen—labored side by side in the deafening mills. "Malnutrition was universal," the committee noted in its report. "The chief articles of diet were oleomargarine, condensed milk, and a cheap meat stew." Factories and housing throughout Lawrence were deemed overcrowded and unsafe.

In the walkout's first days, union organizers rushed to Lawrence. The Industrial Workers of the World (IWW, also known as "Wobblies") sent

Joseph Ettor and Arturo Giovannitti from New York to provide strike management. The pair were soon arrested and confined in jail on trumped-up charges as accessories to murder. The police quickly regretted the arrests, for they only served to draw into their midst "Big Bill" Haywood, a highly regarded and experienced IWW leader. Haywood was met at the Lawrence railroad station by a crowd of fifteen thousand.

The winter of 1912 proved an especially harsh time for a strike. Union leaders and families made the difficult decision to send workers' children to live with families in New York, Philadelphia, and elsewhere. This exodus was interrupted on February 24, when police took nearly 150 children and their parents into custody, provoking yet another round of negative publicity for the authorities. By March 18, the strike was settled. Exhausted workers had won a one-cent-per-hour pay increase and other concessions.

A photograph of a young girl marching in a Lawrence strike parade and carrying a banner that declared, "We want bread and roses, too," inspired James Oppenheim, a radical poet and novelist, to memorialize the strike in verse:

> As we come marching, marching, we bring the greater days
> The rising of the women is the rising of the race.
> No more the drudge and idler—ten that toil while one reposes
> But a sharing of life's glories: Bread and Roses! Bread and Roses!

76 | 1916

President Woodrow Wilson nominates Boston attorney Louis Brandeis to the U.S. Supreme Court.

AS 1916 OPENED, WAR ACROSS EUROPE DRAGGED ON with a heavy cost in lives, while in the United States, the same war was helping the economy climb out of depression. The son of a Southern minister and the

Brandeis University, Waltham

former president of Princeton University, President Woodrow Wilson led a nation at the crossroads of history. With his glasses and pursed lips, he seemed a man unlikely to challenge convention or take on conflict; instead, Wilson fit perfectly the mild image of the history professor he once had been.

In a meteoric political career, however, Wilson had regularly defied expectations. At Princeton, Wilson had fought old-line snobbery in the school's traditional "eating clubs." A Democrat, he was elected in 1910 as governor of New Jersey, and in 1912 as U.S. president, largely on a progressive platform that called for greater regulation of business and improvements in conditions for the common worker. Nevertheless, the nomination on January 28, 1916, of Louis Dembitz Brandeis to the highest court in the land was thoroughly unexpected, even from Wilson.

After the death of Justice Joseph Rucker Lamar, a conservative and a Republican, on January 2, 1916, the nation's business establishment and leading newspapers lobbied heavily for the appointment of former President William Howard Taft, who was then teaching at Yale University as a professor of constitutional law. In contrast to the rotund Taft, the lean Louis Brandeis practiced law in a downtown Boston firm that he had founded in 1879 with Samuel Warren, his Harvard Law School classmate. A Democrat and social activist who almost gleefully took on the banks and trusts,

Brandeis became widely known for his successful defenses of groundbreaking state labor statutes, including minimum-wage laws and laws protecting women and children in the workplace. In 1893, he argued against the West End Railway's plans to lay track across historic Boston Common. Beginning in 1907, Brandeis laid the groundwork for the Savings Bank Life Insurance system, and in 1914, he collected his legal writings under a provocative title: *Other People's Money, and How the Bankers Use It.*

As if all this were not affront enough, however, "the attorney for the people" was also a Jew, born in Louisville, Kentucky, of parents who had emigrated from Prague. A prominent Zionist, Brandeis eloquently supported the movement to create a Jewish homeland in what was then British-controlled Palestine. Newswire reports described the Brandeis nomination to the Supreme Court—the first ever for a Jew—as "a bomb."

As a Senate subcommittee painstakingly examined his fitness for office, Brandeis endured attacks on his professional conduct and his qualifications—but he famously "said nothing at all." Even as Harvard College President A. Lawrence Lowell joined with others in attacking the nomination, Brandeis drew praise from union members, progressives, and immigrants of all stripes. Charles Eliot, President Emeritus of Harvard, joined the fray on the side of his old friend and declared, "The rejection by the Senate of [the Brandeis] nomination to the Supreme Court would be a grave misfortune for the whole legal profession, the court, all American business and the country." On June 1, 1916, the Senate confirmed Brandeis on a party-line vote, 47 to 22.

In 1915, at the invitation of Mayor James Michael Curley, Brandeis became the first Jew to deliver the city's annual Fourth of July oration at Faneuil Hall. In his address, Brandeis hailed the American principle of equality for all and called for social justice. "What are the American ideals?" he asked his audience. "They are the development of the individual for his own and the common good; the development of the individual through liberty, and the attainment of the common good through democracy and social justice." From the bench of the U.S. Supreme Court, where he served from 1916 until he retired in 1939, Brandeis upheld those principles, often in dissenting opinions with Brahmin jurist Oliver Wendell Holmes. Brandeis died in 1941. Founded in 1948 with the financial underwriting of American Jewish leaders, Brandeis University in Waltham, Massachusetts, was named in his honor.

77

A tank holding 2 million gallons of molasses bursts in the North End.

ON AN UNSEASONABLY WARM WINTER AFTERNOON, children in Boston's North End finished their lunches and began returning to school for their afternoon classes. Along Commercial Street, dogs roamed aimlessly and pedestrians coursed distractedly. The elevated train squealed through the air above the neighborhood streets. In that era, automobiles were a rare sight. Much more common were teamsters on delivery rounds.

In offices above the street, men and women heard a muffled rumble from outside. They paused at their work and looked up from their desks. The sound was different from the usual city noises of trains and traffic. It roared, then whistled like the wind.

All at once, windows were blackened as if a curtain had been drawn across the front of buildings. A brown liquid with a sickly sweet odor began pouring in through open windows and broken panes. The world was coming to an end in a sticky flood of molasses.

On the corner of Foster and Commercial streets, a ninety-foot tank filled with more than 2 million gallons of molasses weighing over fourteen thousand tons had exploded. The liquid was being used by the Purity Distilling Company for the production of munitions. (Making rum with the molasses was illegal; Massachusetts had recently ratified the Eighteenth Amendment, prohibiting the manufacture, sale, or transportation of intoxicating liquors.)

According to eyewitnesses, the crackle of a thousand machine guns rang out near the tank just after 12:30 P.M. on January 15, 1919. As it ruptured with a tremendous force, the steel structure shattered into bits of deadly shrapnel. One piece sliced through a girder supporting the elevated railway like so much cheese.

Cascading from the ruptured tank, a wave of molasses rose thirty feet in the air. Couples walking arm in arm were torn apart, with death claiming one while the other miraculously escaped. The molasses swept through the street and carried off its victims without pity. Like flies caught on sticky flypaper, the more people and animals struggled, the tighter the molasses held them in its grip. Some were not immediately drowned but died from suffocation after molasses plugged their nostrils.

Firefighters pulled unrecognizable brown forms from the molasses. The sticky substance swirled and bubbled in the street as rescue teams—with molasses up to their waists—struggled to separate the living from the dead. Water from high-pressure hoses was useless to move the mess, but some ingenious firefighters discovered that seawater cut through it. They were finally able to wash the sickening mess off the streets and into the nearby harbor.

In the bizarre flood, twenty-one people died and 150 were injured. In court, expert witnesses testified that the holding tank was improperly designed and structurally inadequate for the volume of molasses stored inside it. The Purity Distilling Company was ordered to pay more than $1 million in claims to survivors and property owners.

78

1919

The Boston police strike gains Gov. Calvin Coolidge national prominence.

IN AUGUST 1919, THIRTEEN HUNDRED BOSTON police officers voted to enroll their fraternal group, the Boston Social Club, in the American Federation of Labor (AFL). The pro-union vote followed complaints of low wages, unsanitary working conditions, and mandatory overtime with insufficient compensation. The police commissioner, who was against the union, immediately forbade the officers from being members of any organization except veterans' organizations. City officials subsequently found eight officers guilty of disobeying the anti-union rule.

A strike order was called for September 9, effective with the evening roll call. That night, fewer than 10 percent of the force arrived for duty. As darkness gathered, Boston was plunged into chaos. Robbery and looting were rampant.

To ensure the maintenance of order, stalwart citizens prepared to make sacrifices. The Harvard College football coach volunteered his players as police substitutes, saying, "To hell with football if men are needed." In the meantime, union sympathizers surrounded police stations to chant their support for strikers and heckle any picket-crossing scabs. National Guard officers on duty in South Boston opened fire on pro-union demonstrators, killing two and wounding seven others. In Scollay Square, National Guard cavalry charged a crowd; one woman was shot and a man lay dead.

Despite his noted indifference, Massachusetts Gov. Coolidge received the lion's share of public credit for breaking the back of the strike. The diffident and laconic Yankee held firmly to a basic principle: "There is no right," he said, "to strike against the public safety by anybody, anywhere, anytime."

Ironically, the man perhaps most responsible for restoring peace in Boston was AFL president Samuel Gompers. On September 11 he ordered the striking men to return to their posts for the good of all labor causes. A day later, the police union voted to comply with Gompers and public sentiment; the officers reluctantly returned to work, although a few strikers were reinstated by the city.

With the Boston police strike ended, "Honest Cal" was boosted from Beacon Hill to Pennsylvania Avenue. In a year's time, he won election as vice president on the Republican Party's "return to normalcy" ticket with President Warren G. Harding of Ohio. He ascended to the White House in 1923 at Harding's death and handily won reelection in 1924.

79

His short-lived financial empire in ruins, Charles Ponzi of Boston is arrested for fraud.

CHARLES PONZI DID NOT INVENT THE PYRAMID scheme, any more than Harry Houdini created the escape act. Instead, both men imagined and executed remarkably convincing variations of time-tested stunts. Both were immigrants to an America where self-invention, not to mention considerable skills in sleight-of-hand, lent them considerable advantages in the ongoing economic free-for-all that also spawned more socially acceptable confidence men like Rockefeller, Carnegie, and Ford.

Carlo Ponsi was born in Parma, Italy, in 1883. According to legend, he was shipped to Boston in 1903 by relatives who had grown weary of paying his gambling debts. Like Harry Houdini (who was born Ehrich Weiss in Budapest in 1874), Charles Ponzi made his new name a lasting legacy in his adopted home. Today, "Ponzi schemes" include a whole bag of financial tricks that are otherwise known as "pyramid schemes." The principle involved with such chicanery is fairly simple: to pay Paul, borrow from Peter; to pay Peter, borrow from a third; and so on. Pyramid scheme investors are first drawn in by fantastic promises of short-term financial return. Only those who cash out early, however, manage to see any reward. The ones who do "get rich quick" unwittingly become the gilded bait for waves upon waves of deluded "investors" who trust that their money will grow tremendously in value. Ultimately, either the investors stop arriving or payouts end from lack of cash. (Sometimes both occur.) A panic run on "the bank" usually sends the whole scheme crashing down like a house of cards, although often only after the perpetrator has fled.

After arriving in Boston, Charles Ponzi began to acquire an education in forgery and petty theft over the next ten years, with stops in New York,

Providence, and Montreal. He eventually returned to Massachusetts after several stretches in state and federal jails. After World War I ended in 1918, Wall Street, along with the rest of the country, felt itself in the first throes of a historic bull market. Steel companies and automobile makers were busy transforming the landscape and reaping bounties for their owners. Highborn Yankees and hardscrabble immigrants alike read thrilling newspaper accounts of fortunes won apparently overnight. America truly was a place where dreams came true and miracles happened every day.

In December 1919, Ponzi incorporated the Securities Exchange Company and worked from a small office on School Street in Boston with a view of City Hall. His method for transforming paupers into princes was to rely on a strange oversight in foreign currency laws. Owing to fluctuations in exchange rates, international reply coupons that were purchased in post offices overseas for one or two cents could be cashed in the United States for as much as three times their original price. The difference was real enough, and on the face of it, the transaction was not illegal.

For the next eight months, Charles Ponzi relied on this simple but effective cover story to rake in an estimated $15 million in "investments." He first promised to double any individual deposit in ninety days, then shortened the period by half, all at a time when banks paid 5 percent interest. In a burst of publicity and acclaim, Ponzi managed to establish an international reputation as a financial wizard. In fact, he was simply operating an elaborate pass-through system for the money he took in and relying on the patience of the greedy to maintain a positive cash flow.

As investigative reporters published the obvious (that there were simply not enough postage coupons printed in a year to cover the sums of money supposedly changing hands), and as dubious government officials caught whiff of approaching disaster, Ponzi remained cool. Owing to either a character flaw or criminal audacity, however, the dapper and diminutive Italian-American lost his fortune and his liberty after making a basic, even obvious misstep: he took the money, but did not run. When caught, Ponzi managed to leave behind only $1.3 million in assets against liabilities of almost $4 million. For his criminal ingenuity, Ponzi received a lengthy prison sentence and was deported in 1934.

80

The Boston Red Sox sell Babe Ruth to the New York Yankees.

OVER THE 1919 BASEBALL SEASON HANGS THE shadow of the "Black Sox" scandal. All but forgotten, however, is that the 1919 season saw a dramatic personal achievement, one that heralded the arrival of a new breed of baseball player: the slugger. In Boston, Babe Ruth, a pitcher-turned-outfielder, had notched a record twenty-nine home runs. Ruth would nearly double that historic mark in the following season, but not as a player for the Red Sox.

A left-handed hitter, George Herman Ruth was built like a cast-iron statue. He stood 6 feet, 2 inches tall and weighed 215 pounds. Born a bartender's son and raised in a Baltimore tenement, the "young Goliath" became the toast of Boston. The baby-faced twenty-three-year-old carefully maneuvered his wide-body Packard through Boston's narrow streets and was recognized wherever he went. In fact, Ruth was lionized as probably no athlete before him had been. Other men were in awe of Ruth; women found him irresistibly attractive.

In the first fifteen years of the modern World Series, the Boston Red Sox had won four titles, more than any other team. Ruth came to the team in 1914, and his tremendous pitching abilities had made the difference in 1916 and 1918, two championship seasons for the Red Sox. In 1916 the home team defeated the Brooklyn Dodgers, four games to one; in the second, grueling game of that matchup, pitcher Babe Ruth gave up just six hits in fourteen innings on the mound to lead the Sox to a 2–1 victory. Two years later, Ruth pitched 29⅔ scoreless innings, a series record, as the Red Sox beat the Cubs, four games to two.

Even the most casual of American baseball fans were aware that the team with Babe Ruth on its side was the one to beat. In a word, Ruth was priceless. Red Sox owner Harry Frazee, however, saw things differently. Before the start of the 1919 season, Ruth demanded to be paid $10,000. Frazee refused, and "the Babe" threatened to sit out the entire year. The pair finally agreed to a $9,000 salary, and before the season ended, they had renegotiated a three-year contract paying Ruth $10,000 a year.

Making money came as easily to Babe Ruth in those days as hitting home runs. As the only baseball player in the league with his own business manager, he managed to pull in thousands at "barnstorming" exhibition games he played across New England. Ruth even invested in a local cigar factory that rolled its product in colorful paper bands printed with his smiling face.

In both attendance and revenues, the 1919 baseball season was the best yet in major-league history. When the season ended, Johnny Igoe, Ruth's manager, chose his moment to demand even more money for his player. Ruth's salary with the Red Sox would now have to be $20,000 or he wouldn't play at all in 1920.

Once more, Harry Frazee refused. A theatrical entrepreneur, he had bought the Red Sox in late 1916. Despite owning a winner, he quickly found himself in financial hot water with impatient creditors. When an upstart American League team in New York began to throw money around, Frazee signaled that Ruth was for sale.

On January 5, 1920, the owners of the New York Yankees promptly snatched up Babe Ruth for $125,000—more than double the price ever before paid a team for one of its ballplayers. In New York, Ruth would get the $20,000 salary he had demanded in Boston. For more than eighty years afterward—until, at last, in 2004—the Red Sox did not win another World Series, a record of defeat that fans blamed on the "Curse of the Bambino."

81

1926

In Auburn, Robert Goddard launches the first liquid-fuel rocket.

SPRING WAS ONLY A FEW DAYS AWAY, BUT SNOW still covered the rolling fields of rural central Massachusetts on March 16, 1926. A Clark University professor of physics was dressed appropriately as he stood in a field in Auburn where his aunt, Effie Ward, owned a farm. His full-length overcoat was buttoned to the neck, with the collar turned up to his ears against a sharp wind. On his feet, his heavy boots were laced well above the ankles. He wore a tweed cap to protect his hairless head and a pair of leather gloves supple enough for delicate handiwork.

With Henry Sachs, a skilled machinist, assisting him, Robert H. Goddard was about to accomplish what his favorite authors, Jules Verne and H. G. Wells, had imagined in their science-fiction novels. In 1898 Goddard read *War of the Worlds* serialized in the *Boston Post* and began to work out the problem of space flight in his head. Also that year, on October 19, the sixteen-year-old Goddard climbed a cherry tree in his Roxbury backyard and was struck by a tremendous idea that he later described in his diary.

"I imagined how wonderful it would be to make [a] device which had even the possibility of ascending to Mars," he wrote. "When I descended the tree . . . existence at last seemed very purposive." Goddard celebrated this moment of spiritual rebirth throughout his life as his "Anniversary Day."

In December 1925 Goddard had successfully tested his revolutionary liquid-fuel rocket in a static testing track at his Clark laboratory. He had already developed the basic principles of modern rocketry. Goddard was the first to recognize that thrust—and thus propulsion—can take place in a vacuum without air to push against. He was also the first to work out the necessary mathematical ratios of energy and thrust for liquid oxygen, liquid hydrogen, and other now common rocket fuels.

That morning in the cold, on March 16, 1926, Goddard and Sachs assembled a rocket motor and fuel tanks. The device, encased in a ten-foot-long tubing, was held in place by a sturdy pipe frame. By noon, Goddard and Sachs were joined by Percy Roope, another Clark physicist, and Esther Goddard, who was to make a motion-picture film of the historic launch. Aunt Effie stayed warm inside her farmhouse and prepared hot malted milks.

In his diary, Goddard recorded that the launch finally occurred at 2:30 P.M. The rocket rose 41 feet and landed 184 feet away in a flight lasting 2.5 seconds. Esther Goddard's camera, which required rewinding after it consumed just 7 seconds of film, unfortunately ran down before ignition. When Goddard wrote to his mentor Charles Abbot of the Smithsonian Institution about the experiment's success, he enclosed a photograph of the empty pipe frame that once had held his invention.

82 | 1927

Nicola Sacco and Bartolomeo Vanzetti are executed.

IN CHARLESTOWN PRISON ON AUGUST 23, 1927, TWO Italian immigrants prepared to go to their deaths in the electric chair. Very few people anywhere truly believed that Nicola Sacco and Bartolomeo Vanzetti were guilty of the crime with which they had been charged and convicted. The more the world agitated for clemency, however, the more the guardians of law and order in Massachusetts became determined to fulfill the court verdict pronounced by Judge Webster Thayer on July 14, 1921.

So that his conscience and the justice system of the commonwealth could appear free from blemish, Gov. Alvan T. Fuller had called for an independent inquiry. Impartial men—the likes of A. Lawrence Lowell, president of Harvard College, and Samuel W. Stratton, president of the Massachusetts Institute of Technology—were asked to serve the commonwealth in its moment of need. The Lowell Committee, as it became known, reviewed what was already well known internationally about the case.

When arrested as "suspicious persons" while riding on a Brockton streetcar on the evening of May 5, 1920, Sacco and Vanzetti were found to be armed—Sacco with a .32 Colt pistol, Vanzetti with a .38 revolver. Both weapons were loaded. At the police station, the men made a number of false statements about their recent movements and about their political affiliations. They reluctantly admitted they were anarchists, members of a violent political movement on the rise in the United States following World War 1.

Police immediately became convinced that the men were involved in an April 20 holdup at the Slater and Morrill Shoe Factory, South Braintree, in which the company paymaster and a security guard were killed and more than $15,000 in cash was taken.

In court the prosecution spun a complicated web to link Sacco and Vanzetti with the crime. Little material evidence was produced. The district attorney primarily relied on the men's behavior at the time of their arrest. Carrying guns and lying to the authorities, he told the court, indicated a "consciousness of guilt" in connection with the holdup and double murder.

Law-abiding citizens had good reason to fear anarchists and to want them executed or otherwise silenced. In September 1920 an anarchist's bomb exploded at the corner of Wall and Broad streets in downtown Manhattan, killing thirty and injuring more than two hundred. "We will destroy to rid the world of your tyrannical institutions!" anarchists thundered at the nation's trembling capitalists. "Long live social revolution! Down with tyranny!"

As for Judge Thayer, he made various statements outside the courtroom that appeared somewhat injudicious. "Did you see what I did with those anarchist bastards the other day? I guess that will hold them for a while!" is the most widely quoted of such remarks. The Lowell Committee determined that Judge Thayer was guilty of a "grave breach of official decorum."

The Lowell Committee also decided that Sacco and Vanzetti were guilty. Clemency was refused. Finally, on August 23, 1927, the two men were executed. "We are proud for death," Sacco wrote in his last hours.

Artists and writers found in the Sacco and Vanzetti case a model for American social injustice in the 1920s. For author John Dos Passos, the injustice showed the United States to be "two nations"—one rich, the other poor; one powerful, the other powerless. Artist Ben Shahn sharply evoked the men's pathetic plight in his 1931 painting titled *Passion of Sacco & Vanzetti.*

83

The Great Hurricane hits, costing millions in damages.

METEOROLOGICALLY SPEAKING, A TROPICAL depression becomes a hurricane when the storm's heaviest winds exceed 65 knots (the equivalent of 75 miles per hour or 120 kilometers per hour). Unusually strong hurricanes with sustained winds blowing between 111 and 130 miles per hour are rated as "category 3" storms. In more recent New England memory, Hurricane Gloria (1985) and Hurricane Bob (1991) were both category 3 storms.

The last category 4 storm—with sustained winds between 131 and 155 miles per hour—swept up the northeastern coast on September 21, 1938. The impact of this greatest of all recorded Massachusetts hurricanes was ferocious: by official count, some 650 people were killed in New England and Long Island. The "Great Hurricane of 1938" did not have a name because not until 1953 were tropical storms given names.

Most of the hurricane's victims were drowned when surging waves and overflowing rivers lifted them off their feet and swept them violently into watery graves. Seaside cottages where families were huddled in fear came away from their foundations. Buildings and occupants were swallowed whole by the churning sea.

Death and destruction in the Great Hurricane of 1938 came from freakish accidents as well. Chimneys collapsed, and automobiles were overturned like children's toys. The Athol River swirled with tapioca from a factory spill at Orange (approximately seventy miles inland). Trees and utility poles were snapped in half as easily as matchsticks. Fifteen percent of all mature timber in New England—enough to build 200,000 homes—was mowed to the ground by the hurricane's winds.

Of course, there were no weather satellites or other high-tech gadgetry to track the Great Hurricane of 1938. Those who remember the storm recall it as striking without warning, though this does not mean it was entirely unexpected. Government meteorologists were aware of an approaching storm, but they had expected it to follow a curling, coastal track that would keep it safely away from land.

According to meteorologists, the conditions that created the Great Hurricane of 1938 (a pair of massive high-pressure weather systems with room enough for an errant depression to squeeze between them) typically occur as often as ten times a year.

84

1939

The Swift River Valley is flooded to create the world's largest man-made source of water.

IN 1895 THE MASSACHUSETTS BOARD OF HEALTH issued a lengthy if inconclusive report on how the state should address metropolitan Boston's persistent water supply problem.

The commonwealth's engineers considered the suitability of water in the Merrimack River and the Charles River (both too polluted); Lake Winnipesaukee in New Hampshire and Sebago Lake in Maine (both too distant and outside Massachusetts); and numerous other alternatives. The Metropolitan Water and Sewerage Board eventually decided to construct a reservoir by diverting a Nashua River tributary.

The Wachusett Reservoir was created with a 64-billion-gallon capacity, yet the need for additional supply was immediately foreseen. By 1928, state engineers began work on what was to be called the Quabbin Reservoir. Four towns in the Swift River Valley of central Massachusetts—Dana, Enfield, Greenwich, and Prescott—were ordered taken by eminent domain.

Massachusetts authorities had picked the location well. The Swift River Valley was chosen for obliteration because it contained no important

businesses and relatively few people. Opposition to the $65 million project did not appreciably slow the project. The timeline for demolition and dam building moved inexorably forward throughout the 1930s.

At the Quabbin Park Cemetery, more than 6,500 bodies were brought from cemeteries across the Swift River Valley and reinterred. The living were not quite so easily relocated. Finally, voters in the four condemned towns held their last town meetings in the spring of 1938. The state legislature subsequently wrote the towns out of existence, effective one minute past midnight, April 28. At the Enfield Town Hall, firemen sponsored a festive ball to mark the occasion. The very last of the valley's remaining families, however, were not gone for another year.

On August 14, 1939, gates to a dam holding back the Swift River were opened, and the Quabbin began to fill. Workers continued to demolish buildings left standing in the district well into 1940. On June 22, 1946, the reservoir reached its capacity of 412 billion gallons and was declared full. Work to create the world's largest artificial domestic water source had finally ended. The Quabbin today covers 39 square miles and has an average depth of 51 feet.

Eerie stories that houses can sometimes be seen through the reservoir's waters are entirely fanciful. During a 1965 drought, however, stone foundation steps emerged through the mud and low water that covered what was once Dana, Massachusetts.

85

Ted Williams bats .406.

IN BASEBALL MORE THAN IN ANY OTHER SPORT, percentages matter. This obsession with statistics is not only a source of endless fascination for fans but also a fundamental element in the game itself. Over the course of a 162-game professional season, baseball managers and their players are as mindful as aluminum-siding salespeople that they are in a numbers game.

On Sunday, September 28, 1941, Boston Red Sox outfielder Ted Williams would have seen printed in newspaper sports sections across the country an extraordinary number. The slugger's batting average (calculated as a ratio of hits to total times at bat) was .400. His other important numbers that day, as the Red Sox prepared for a season-ending doubleheader against the Athletics at Philadelphia, were equally impressive: in 444 at-bats so far that season, Williams had driven in 118 runs and notched 36 home runs.

Only seven major-leaguers in the twentieth century had previously achieved a season batting average above .400. The last to do so was thirty-one-year-old Bill Terry, playing for the 1930 National League New York Giants, who had whacked his way to .401. In his third major-league season with the Red Sox, Ted Williams was just twenty-three years old (hence his popular nickname, "the Kid"). If the "magic number" of .400 held one more day, he would become the youngest player of the modern era to hit .400 or over for the season.

On baseball cards and in the press, baseball hitters' batting averages are typically calculated to just three decimal places. It sounded like quibbling then, but despite the newspapers, Ted Williams was not quite batting .400 on September 28, 1941. Carried out to a fourth decimal place, his average was .3995. Williams had connected regularly throughout September, but at nothing like the pace he had set throughout the summer. In fact, after reaching .411 on September 14, his average had slipped.

For either side, Red Sox or Athletics, the doubleheader to be played on September 28 would have no effect on team standings. The Red Sox had been eliminated from World Series contention two weeks earlier by their archrivals, the Yankees. The Philadelphia Athletics were a last-place team.

In the first game that afternoon, Williams went four-for-five with a home run and three singles and boosted his average to .405. A player more concerned about his place in history might have chosen to protect his average by sitting out the next game. "Never crossed my mind," Williams told *Boston Globe* sportswriter Peter Gammons fifty years later. "I was getting paid, I played. It was as simple as that." For the second game, the slugger went two-for-four. His average rose another notch, to .406.

For the record, Ted Williams's career statistics read as follows: .344 lifetime batting average; 521 home runs; 1,839 runs batted in; and 2,654 total hits. His average fell below .300 only in 1959, when he slumped to .254. Altogether, he played nineteen seasons for the Boston Red Sox, with time out for military service in World War II and the Korean War.

Ted Williams played his last game at Fenway Park on September 28, 1960. In his final professional at-bat, he hit an eighth-inning, two-run homer. Williams trotted around the bases as the 10,454 fans cheered. Then he disappeared inside the dugout without further fuss. The Red Sox eventually won, 5–4.

86

1942

The Cocoanut Grove nightclub fire kills 492.

THE DEAD, THE DYING, AND THE BARELY LIVING were rushed into Boston City Hospital throughout the long night of November 28, 1942, until they numbered in the hundreds. A weary physician finally telephoned the police and begged authorities that no more of the dead be brought to his crowded emergency ward. The doctor's desperate call came less than an hour after the first fire victims began to arrive.

Many of those relaxing in the Melody Lounge at the Cocoanut Grove that night were attending what had been scheduled as a victory party for the Boston College football team. Instead, they mourned a devastating loss by the Eagles to rival Holy Cross, 55–12. Young men and women poured into the popular spot at Piedmont Street and Broadway in South Boston. Off-duty servicemen and holiday revelers eagerly joined them for a drink or a dance.

According to some reports, the devastating fire may have been started accidentally by Stanley Tomaszweski, a sixteen-year-old busboy who was working illegally at the Cocoanut Grove. With his father out of work, the $2.47 wage plus tips that Stanley earned nightly was crucial to his family's support. Holding a burning match to help him see, Tomaszweski had diligently replaced a lightbulb hung on a decorative potted palm. According to witnesses, he walked away unwittingly as a smoldering palm frond ignited the ceiling's satin fabric.

An investigation, however, labeled the fire of unknown origin and suggested that the cause could also have been "alcoholic fumes, inflammable insecticides, motion picture film scraps, electric wiring, gasoline or fuel oil fumes, refrigerant gases, [or] flameproofing chemicals."

The fire—actually a large volume of inflammable gases—raced from its starting point to a distant doorway 225 feet away in fewer than five minutes. Every exit available was partially or completely blocked: a revolving door was jammed; four doors were locked; two recently installed doors opened inward and were useless. Many victims succumbed to poisonous fumes and were not actually burned alive. Indeed, many of those pulled from the inferno were, strangely, not scarred by flames.

Like the *Titanic* disaster, the tragedy of the Cocoanut Grove fire spurred important reforms. Fire codes in Boston and across the country were largely rewritten. In addition, doctors learned to treat severe burn victims more successfully.

87 1944

The computer age dawns in Cambridge laboratories.

THE MARK I, A CALCULATING MACHINE MORE THAN fifty feet long, was an entirely new species of electro-mechanical device. Its progenitors were a team of scientists from Harvard University, IBM, and the U.S. Navy, led by Harvard's Howard Aiken. More nineteenth-century "analytical engine" than twentieth-century electrical computer, the clumsy creature was even more clumsily named the Harvard-IBM Mark I Automatic Sequence Controlled Calculator (ASCC).

Mark I was programmed in a digital code that was punched onto paper tape and cards. Counterwheels for calculations were electromechanical, with electrical connections between units. The "memory" consisted of seventy-two counters and sixty switches.

According to Aiken, the Mark I owed its conception to the desire to minimize time and effort in ever more sophisticated mathematical calculations. As science had increased its ability to measure the physical universe throughout the nineteenth and early twentieth centuries, so the need had grown for accurate computation of lengthy differential equations and other complex formulas.

Concurrently in 1944, the Massachusetts Institute of Technology agreed to build for the U.S. Navy a new generation of real-time aircraft flight simulators. Jay Forrester and other scientists at the school's Servomechanisms Lab at first pursued a clumsy analog device. In 1946 they substituted for that notion "Whirlwind," a digital computer that, when construction was completed in 1951, filled thirty-one hundred square feet or several large rooms.

During the cold war, American military leaders pressed for computer calculating systems capable of monitoring the nation's growing arsenal of aircraft loaded with atomic weapons as well as guarding against attack

Jay Forrester

by Soviet planes. To permit real-time calculations, Whirlwind relied on advances in cathode-ray tube (CRT) memory. Project scientists gradually grew dissatisfied with CRT memory, however, and by 1953 the MIT team had developed a substitute using magnetic cores to store computer memory more reliably and more easily. Computers have long since left the laboratory, of course, and their numbers have increased to epidemic proportions.

88

1945

Under indictment for mail fraud, James Michael Curley is reelected mayor of Boston.

BORN NOVEMBER 20, 1874, OF IMMIGRANTS FROM Galway, in an prototypical coldwater flat on Northampton Street in Roxbury, James Michael Curley was orphaned at ten years old. At eleven, the boy took his

Statue of James Michael Curley

first job, hawking newspapers on Washington Street. His political career began in 1899 with a term as Boston city councillor. He later served as Boston mayor, Massachusetts state representative, Massachusetts governor, and U.S. congressman.

Of all his titles, Curley arguably cherished "Mr. Mayor" the most. Curley was first elected to the chief executive's post at City Hall in 1914 and was defeated and reelected several times over the next thirty years.

James Michael Curley's most memorable election battle was the one fought in 1945. He already held office as U.S. representative for the state's Eleventh District in Charlestown, but the lure of City Hall proved irresistible.

Indeed, not even indictment by a federal grand jury for mail fraud could stop him from pursuing a fourth term as "His Honor." That it also did not prevent Bostonians from voting for him in record numbers is not surprising either. He won nineteen of twenty-two city wards with a larger margin than any mayoral candidate before him. Conveniently for his mayoral campaign, the congressman's trial in a Washington, D.C., court did not begin until December 1945. The indictments charged that Curley had served with two others as officers of the Engineer's Group, a mining syndicate in name only; the several partners in the Engineer's Group were accused of misrepresenting themselves to potential clients and spending retainers recklessly. A 1943 series of indictments against them was dismissed on technicalities, but the government rebounded with new charges that stuck.

Shortly after his inauguration in Boston, Curley returned to Washington and received the jury's verdict: guilty. The seventy-one-year-old politician faced a maximum sentence of forty-seven years and a $19,000 fine; he received a sentence of six to eighteen months and a fine of $1,000.

Curley refused to resign either from Congress or as mayor of Boston. He tried his best, in fact, to behave as if nothing had happened. In 1947 an appeals court upheld his conviction. Justice had at last caught up with James Michael Curley.

Even as his lawyers railed that jail would prove a death sentence for their ailing client, Mayor Curley went to the federal penitentiary in Danbury, Connecticut, on June 26, 1947. Later that year, just days before Thanksgiving, President Harry Truman commuted his sentence. Two days after leaving prison, the mayor was back in his City Hall office. He completed his term but was never elected to office again.

89 | 1950

A holdup of a Brink's armored car nets Boston thieves $2.7 million.

SEVEN MEN ENTERED OFFICES OF THE BRINK'S company at 165 Prince Street in Boston's North End just after 6:30 P.M. on January 17, 1950. They converged on a counting room, where employees were working diligently, tagging heavy sacks of cash and payroll checks and entering figures in ledger books. The seven men waited for their victims to take notice of them. Finally, one of the robbers spoke impatiently: "Hands up!"

Site of the Brink's robbery, Boston

The Brink's employees turned and saw a strange and frightening sight: each of the seven men was identically dressed in chauffeur's cap, pea coat, and dark trousers. All wore flabby, hideous rubber masks like the sort sold at carnivals and joke shops.

After they had opened the office's principal vault, the Brink's employees were tied hand and foot and their mouths were taped tightly shut. The masked gunmen then tore at money sacks, sorting out worthless checks from hard cash as well as "good" (used) money from "bad" money (new bills in serial order that would be easy to trace). One of the men worked frantically but unsuccessfully to pry open a plain metal money box.

In less than an hour, the thieves prepared to leave. They loaded sack after sack of loot onto a waiting truck. At 7:27 P.M., an alarm finally sounded. Within minutes, Boston police and a few ambitious journalists converged on the garage and offices at the corner of Commercial and Prince streets. The excitement and confusion created a chaotic crime scene, and much of the evidence was disturbed.

At first, the official estimate of the take was $100,000—but by the time of the late news, it was up to $1 million. The statement of a Boston police superintendent at a 2:00 A.M. press conference made journalists and the public gawk in awe: $1 million in cash and $500,000 in securities were believed missing from Brink's. Left behind, police estimated, was another $1 million in cash, including a General Electric payroll of $880,000 in the metal money box with the stubborn lock. Later the tally mounted further: gone were more than $1.2 million in currency and more than $1.5 million in checks, money orders, and securities. Until the Brink's robbery, the largest single robbery of hard cash in modern U.S. history had been $427,000, stolen from the Rubble Ice Company in Brooklyn, New York, in 1932.

In a race with the statute of limitations over the next six years, the Boston Police Department and the Federal Bureau of Investigation spent close to $29 million tracking the robbers. Law officials attempted to interview every known criminal in greater Boston. Convinced that the robbery was an inside job, Brink's administered lie-detector tests to the victimized employees of 165 Prince Street.

In December 1955, fewer than three weeks before the Brink's gang members would have been beyond the hand of the law, Joseph James "Specs" O'Keefe began to yield to FBI pressure. A career Boston criminal who had spent most of the five years since the robbery in jail on one charge or another, "Specs" was straining under a mountain of legal bills. Despite repeated pleas for help, O'Keefe had received next to nothing from his partners in crime.

On January 6, 1956, with eleven days remaining, "Specs" O'Keefe started his confession. Eighteen were tried and convicted that August and sent to Walpole State Prison for long terms. In July 1971 Tony Pino, the last of the living Brink's robbers, was paroled after serving a fifteen-year stretch in Walpole.

90

1953

The world's first successful human kidney transplant operation is performed.

IN A NEWSPAPER PHOTOGRAPH, THE HERRICK TWINS stand at the front entrance of the old Peter Bent Brigham Hospital (now part of Brigham and Women's Hospital) on Huntington Avenue. The pair wear matching gray overcoats; both Ronald and Richard have their hands thrust deep in their pockets, presumably to ward off a sharp December wind. It was a sunny day, in any case. The twins cast identical sharp shadows on the portico pavement.

Handsome young men with neatly brushed dark hair, the twenty-three-year-old Herricks appear equally at ease and in good health. But careful scrutiny of their faces and frames points to a fatal difference. Ronald is thin, with chiseled facial features. Richard's upper body is larger, and his face is swollen. His bloated condition, known as edema or dropsy, a retention of body fluids, was a telltale symptom of kidney dysfunction, which was slowly killing him.

Humans are born with a pair of kidneys and can survive with only one fully functioning. If both kidneys become damaged by disease or injury, however, the body will suffer massively debilitating impairment.

In 1953, the "mechanical kidney," which cleansed the body of waste and excess fluids by a process called "dialysis," was a new and relatively untested treatment. At the Brigham, physicians and researchers had experimented with transplanting healthy human kidneys, but without success. In the first such operations, the kidney was transplanted into the patient's thigh so it could be removed quickly and without major abdominal surgery in case of problems.

The Brigham surgeons learned the hard way that the body will attack a transplanted organ as it would any foreign object. Dr. Joseph E. Murray, a native of Milford, Massachusetts, and a skilled plastic surgeon, sought ways to short-circuit this rejection process. He theorized that it would not happen if an organ were transplanted from one identical twin to another. In a sense, such an operation would trick the body's natural defenses.

On December 23, 1954, Dr. Murray removed a kidney from the healthy Ronald Herrick and transplanted it into his brother, Richard. The operation's success led Murray and other researchers to continue transplanting organs and later to develop treatments that would prevent the body from rejecting new organs. At first, low-dose radiation was used to fight rejection; then, in 1962, the first immunosuppressive drugs appeared. For his pioneering medical work, Dr. Murray shared the 1990 Nobel Prize in Medicine with E. Donnall Thomas, a Seattle-based researcher.

After the transplant, Richard Herrick lived seven years before succumbing to congestive heart failure brought on by his original kidney disease. Since that first kidney transplant, such lifesaving operations have become almost commonplace.

91

1954

Malcolm X opens Muhammad's Mosque 11.

THE MAN WHO RETURNED TO THE STREETS OF Roxbury and Dorchester for the first time in seven years was entirely transformed. Malcolm Little, who had served seven years in Charlestown Prison and Norfolk Prison Colony for burglary, was reborn as Malcolm X, a minister in the Nation of Islam. He exchanged his "slave name" for "X," indicating the unknown African tribe of his ancestors. He also adopted the Muslim sect's strict rules of behavior and personal habits.

In Boston, Malcolm X began to preach the fiery message of Hon. Elijah Muhammad, then Nation of Islam's leader, among the city's African American community. The principal teachings at that time rested on a belief in the racial superiority of Africans and a great fury over the mistreatment they had endured in America and elsewhere from white people, whom Elijah Muhammad considered a race of devils.

Malcolm X also spoke powerfully to his audiences of the injustices of slavery, segregation, and poverty. Among those who listened most intently to Malcolm X was Louis Walcott, the New York–born son of a single mother from Barbados; he had grown up on Roxbury's Shawmut Avenue.

Black separatism was not a new idea to either Malcolm X or Louis Walcott. At meetings of the Universal Negro Improvement Association at the Toussaint Louverture Hall on Tremont Street, a young Walcott heard

Muhammad's Mosque II, Dorchester

Marcus Garvey call on African Americans to support a "Back to Africa" movement. Malcolm X, who was born and spent his early years in Omaha, Nebraska, was likewise impressed by "Garveyism." His father, a Baptist minister, had been an outspoken member of the Universal Negro Improvement Association.

At Boston's English High School, Louis Walcott distinguished himself as a student, athlete, and musician. As a track star, his abilities in the relay consistently made English a winner in school athletics throughout the late 1940s. As a violinist, Walcott won trophies for his excellent playing and even performed on television for *The Ted Mack Original Amateur Hour*. With his brother Alvin (today a highly regarded jazz musician) on piano, Louis Walcott gave popular music recitals. He even proved talented as a calypso singer and was an understudy to Harry Belafonte.

In 1954 Malcolm X founded Muhammad's Mosque II at 10 Washington Street, Dorchester. Louis Walcott converted to the Nation of Islam a year later and become Malcolm X's assistant. He was known as Louis X until Elijah Muhammad later renamed him Louis Farrakhan. Malcolm X was reassigned to organize a Nation of Islam temple in New York City, and ultimately Louis Farrakhan rose to replace him as minister of Mosque II.

Over time, Malcolm X changed his beliefs, becoming less militant; a pilgrimage to Mecca convinced him of the possibility of peace among the world's races. He fell out of favor with Elijah Muhammad, broke away from the Nation of Islam, converted to orthodox Islam, and formed the Organization for Afro-American Unity. Shortly thereafter, in 1965, he was assassinated.

Louis Farrakhan has been more steadfast in his radical convictions. He remained loyal to the Nation of Islam even after allegations surfaced that Elijah Muhammad had broken his own codes of asceticism by having sexual relations with several of his secretaries. Today Farrakhan is the sect's leader throughout the United States.

92

1957

The basis for an oral contraceptive is discovered at the Worcester Foundation for Experimental Biology.

IN 1950, MARGARET SANGER, A FEMINIST, NURSE, and advocate of family planning, joined Katharine Dexter McCormick, a philanthropist who was the second woman to graduate from the Massachusetts Institute of Technology, in an effort to encourage development of a safe, easy, and reliable method of contraception.

The two women sought out Dr. Gregory Pincus, cofounder of the Worcester Foundation for Experimental Biology and an expert in mammalian reproduction. With a check from McCormick for $40,000—the first installment on what grew to nearly $2 million in such gifts made under the umbrella of Sanger's International Planned Parenthood Foundation—

Dr. Pincus began research with his colleagues Dr. John Rock, a Harvard professor of gynecology, and Dr. Min Chueh Chang, an authority on fertilization.

The Worcester Foundation research teams tested dozens of synthetic compounds on rats and rabbits. These efforts eventually led in 1954 to the discovery of an artificial steroid hormone. Depending on the dosage, the hormone was capable either of increasing a woman's chance of conceiving or of preventing ovulation altogether.

By 1957 the Worcester Foundation announced that an oral contraceptive—a white pill the size of an aspirin tablet—had been clinically tested on women in Boston, Puerto Rico, and Haiti with great success. In April 1960 the pill—trademarked as Enovid—was approved for use by the U.S. Food and Drug Administration. Despite common side effects such as bloating and dizziness, "the Pill" quickly became a popular method of birth control around the world.

Following its introduction, the Pill provided ammunition for the sexual revolution of the 1960s. Once women became freed from the constraints of reproductive biology, they could begin to behave differently. A woman using the Pill saw herself as sexually independent; previously, only men had enjoyed that type of freedom.

The Worcester Foundation scientists did not foresee the Pill's impact on sexual mores, nor did they even ask themselves about the potential for such social impact. As a Catholic, Dr. Rock even found himself under attack from the church's hierarchy for violating God's will. Dr. Chang, for his part, said that he considered himself only a basic research scientist with a specialty in fertility. He was interested in population control, not changes in human sexual behavior. "We're scientists and we did it for curiosity," he said. "It was not for people to have a good time."

93 | 1960

Massachusetts Sen. John Fitzgerald Kennedy is elected the thirty-fifth U. S. president.

THE KENNEDY ADMINISTRATION, SEEN THROUGH rose-colored glasses, was an era of Jack's charm and Jackie's elegance. In this "Camelot," the White House was tastefully redecorated and Pearl Buck and Robert Frost were invited to dinner. The youngest elected president in American history, a handsome man brimming with wit and vigor, led the nation to a New Frontier. Meanwhile, his children played hide-and-seek in the Oval Office.

It would not require X-ray vision, however, to see through to Camelot's dark underside. In a winning campaign tactic, the decorated war hero had condemned the Eisenhower administration for permitting a "missile gap" to open between the United States and the Soviet Union. Once in office, he confronted military enemies, both real and imagined, in Vietnam, Cuba, and Berlin. For two weeks in October 1962, nuclear war became a possibility, not just a remote threat.

The 1960 election, which put John Fitzgerald Kennedy in the White House, virtually redefined American politics. Television, particularly a series of broadcast debates, was credited with giving the warm and affable Kennedy a distinct advantage over his Republican opponent. Viewed through the camera lens, at least, Richard Nixon was much less attractive. Ever since, presidential aspirants have risen and fallen according to their ability to project a winning television image.

Virtually forgotten is that Kennedy confronted early in his candidacy a question unthinkable today: whether a Roman Catholic could or even should be elected to the nation's highest office. How Kennedy won over the doubters and even some of the bigots makes a remarkable study.

John F. Kennedy's birthplace, Brookline

At the turn of the century, John "Honey Fitz" Fitzgerald, Rose Kennedy's father, had pretty well disproved the idea that a Catholic and an Irishman never could become mayor of the city of Boston. After he was elected mayor, both Irish and Italian candidates in the predominantly Catholic cities of the Northeast also entered politics and rose to power, voted in by the sheer numbers of those who shared their ancestry and religion.

Across the country, however, on the Midwestern prairies and in the southern hills, bigotry against "papists" was almost as strong as hatred of blacks. Many feared that a Catholic president might betray the United States in favor of the commands of the Roman pope.

In Wisconsin, in September 1959, the Kennedy presidential campaign began in earnest. It swiftly met with anti-Catholic prejudice. "I can't vote for Kennedy," registered Democrats around the state declared. "He's a Catholic."

For its primary polls, the *Milwaukee Journal* divided voters into three categories: Democrat, Republican, and Catholic. The votes were counted according to the candidates' names, and Kennedy received more popular votes than any candidate in the state's history. He had soundly beaten Midwesterner Hubert Humphrey on his own turf, but Kennedy had noticeably failed to carry the state's four predominantly Protestant districts.

Kennedy faced a final grueling test next in West Virginia, where registered voters were 95 percent Protestant and the latest polls showed Humphrey ahead by nearly two to one. On the campaign trail, the Massachusetts senator asked a question daunting for even the most hardened West Virginians: "Did forty million Americans lose their right to run for the presidency on the day they were baptized as Catholics?" In a not so subtle reminder of his record as a war hero, he declared, "Nobody asked me if I was a Catholic when I joined the United States Navy."

The Appalachian Mountain state's Democratic primary became a vote for tolerance (i.e., for Kennedy) or for intolerance. That Hubert Humphrey was an impeccably tolerant man made little difference, and Kennedy swept West Virginia by 60 percent to 40 percent. In November the Democratic Party candidate defeated Richard Nixon by fewer than 120,000 votes out of approximately 69 million cast, but the point was made: Less than 60 years after his grandfather proved that an Irish Catholic could be elected mayor of Boston, John Fitzgerald Kennedy proved that an Irish Catholic could be elected president of the United States.

94

1962

The "Boston Strangler" begins a twenty-one-month spree of rape and murder.

THIRTEEN WOMEN, RANGING IN AGE FROM NINETEEN to eighty-five, shared a common death at the hands of the Boston Strangler. His methods terrorized Bostonians for an agonizing period from June 1962 until January 1964.

The Boston Strangler gained access to his victims' dwellings apparently without forced entry, and when he had chosen the appropriate moment, he attacked viciously. The killer typically tied his victim to her bed, where he raped her repeatedly. Then he strangled her with her hosiery, which he tied in a trademark bow under her chin. He also beat one woman with a lead pipe and stabbed two women: one with a jackknife, another twenty-two times with a fork.

To the public's horror, the Boston Strangler seemed to come and go at will. He even managed to strike on the day following President John Kennedy's assassination. Massachusetts Attorney General Edward Brooke organized a special Boston Strangler investigative bureau in an attempt to solve the crimes. (In 1966, Brooke became the first African American elected to the U.S. Senate since Reconstruction.)

In early 1965, police arrested Albert De Salvo for breaking and entering. The Chelsea native was sent for examination to the state's mental hospital at Bridgewater. After De Salvo reported to his guards that he was hearing voices, he was committed to Bridgewater indefinitely.

Boston Police remembered Albert De Salvo as the "Measuring Man" who had seduced and sexually abused a series of women in the late 1950s. Claiming to represent a Hollywood talent agency, the smooth-talking "Measuring Man" carried a clipboard and measuring tape and gained entry to women's homes to record their "vital statistics." Arrested on an unrelated charge in March 1960, De Salvo confessed to being the Measuring Man, but the police did not consider him a dangerous sex criminal because the attacks were not violent. De Salvo served eleven months of a two-year sentence on a simple breaking-and-entering conviction and was released in April 1962.

At Bridgewater, De Salvo began telling a fellow inmate, George Nassar, about a series of grotesque murders he had committed. Nassar, a Mattapan gas station attendant, was himself charged in a brutal slaying and was even suspected to be the Boston Strangler himself. Eventually he told his lawyer about the strange conversations with De Salvo.

Nassar's lawyer was thirty-two-year-old F. Lee Bailey. The up-and-coming defense attorney conducted a series of interviews with De Salvo, who revealed to him details in the Strangler murders that were otherwise known only to police.

With Bailey representing him, De Salvo pleaded not guilty by reason of insanity to a series of rape charges unrelated to the Strangler killings. In his account of the case, Bailey wrote that he simply wanted De Salvo to wind up in a psychiatric hospital rather than a prison. The jury, however, returned guilty verdicts on all counts.

For lack of evidence, no charges were ever formally brought against De Salvo for the Boston Strangler crimes. In 1973 he was murdered in his Walpole prison cell.

95 | 1971

Ray Tomlinson, a scientist in Cambridge, sends the first e-mail message.

"WHAT HATH GOD WROUGHT?" TAPPED CHARLESTOWN, Massachusetts, native Samuel F. B. Morse in 1844 in the first publicly transmitted telegraph message from Washington, D.C., to Baltimore. "Watson, come here!" cried Alexander Bell from his Boston garret in 1876, marking the first time a human voice was carried over wire. Ray Tomlinson typed "QWERTYUIOP" on a computer keyboard in Cambridge in 1971, dispatching to unknown recipients what we now recognize as the first electronic mail message, or e-mail.

Maybe yes. And maybe not.

Thirty years later, even Tomlinson himself wasn't sure when he sent the message, or to whom, and even exactly what it was he wrote. What is certain, however, is that in the first message, he included the @ symbol in order to direct it to the intended destination, the @ sign separating the user's name from the host computer name. "In English, the @ sign is obvious," Tomlinson recalled in 2001 for the CNET news service on the thirtieth anniversary of e-mail. "Being the only preposition on the English keyboard, it just made sense."

At first called "net notes," or simply "mail," the first e-mail was sent via the ARPAnet, a computer network developed for the U.S. Department of Defense's Advanced Research Projects Agency (ARPA). A forerunner of the Internet, ARPAnet was an elaborate solution to a fairly simple problem: how to transmit data and other electronic information safely and reliably over remote distances. Relying on "packet switching," a variation of "message switching" or "store-and-forward switching" that dated to telegraphy, engineers built a series of secure electronic "post offices," where messages were sent at random, to be stored for subsequent re-transmission along the most efficient possible routes. High transmission speeds made the communication appear to be in real time. Military strategists trusted this "hardened" network to perform under extreme circumstances, even throughout a nuclear war.

According to Tomlinson, he employed a pair of complementary programs in order to send the first e-mail. "SNDMSG" allowed him to compose a message to be placed in the "mailbox" of another user on a time-shared computer network. To send the file data (or "mail") to the other computer, he modified an existing "file transfer protocol" (or FTP) and created CPYNET, an incremental improvement over earlier systems known as READMAIL. Thus was the first "killer app" conceived in the electronic womb.

As networked computing gradually became a global and commercial phenomenon, e-mail transformed business and personal correspondence by vastly improving the efficiency of written communication. The ability to transfer other kinds of data files—such as image, audio, and video files—has resulted in a world where data changes hands more readily and effortlessly than ever before. Further, as Ray Tomlinson himself has noted, e-mail also allows people to go to others they do not personally know and request information from them.

In the early years of the twenty-first century, Cambridge-based Forrester Research has estimated, more than half of all Americans use e-mail daily, typically for about 30 minutes—or roughly two-thirds of the 45 minutes' time they spend talking on telephones. To its great advantage, e-mail combines the immediacy of a telephone call with the asynchronous communication of an ordinary "snail mail" letter. It's hard to imagine life without it, although all of us could live probably with a lot less "spam."

96

1972

*Nixon 49, America 1 —
Massachusetts is the
only state to vote for
George McGovern.*

A COLOR-KEYED MAP SHOWING ELECTORAL VOTES in the 1972 presidential elections looks like a jigsaw puzzle missing a small but essential piece. The votes for every state but one are one color, assigned to the incumbent Republican president, Richard Nixon.

The missing piece is that fiftieth state: Massachusetts. The commonwealth's voters contradicted their compatriots and voted for the president's Democratic opponent, Sen. George McGovern. No American election since 1936, when Franklin Roosevelt overwhelmingly defeated Alf Landon, had ended with as lopsided a decision.

According to the final published tallies, Nixon won the national popular vote by 61 percent to 37 percent (47,170,000 to 29,171,000). In the Electoral College, the margin was even wider, with Nixon receiving 520 votes to McGovern's 17. Massachusetts accounted for 14 of the Democrat's votes, with the District of Columbia, then voting in its first presidential election, adding another 3. In the commonwealth's popular vote, McGovern won decisively, with 1,332,000 votes (54 percent) to Nixon's 1,112,000 (45 percent).

Richard Nixon and George McGovern held fundamentally different political views. They saw government's responsibilities and America's international role from opposite ends of the spectrum. Nixon had shown reluctance to withdraw U.S. troops from Vietnam, while McGovern was a long-standing opponent of continued American military involvement there.

From his position on the left, McGovern also called for a guaranteed annual income—essentially, a plan to redistribute wealth. In 1973,

President Nixon had implemented wage and price controls, yet the Republican remained a solid ally of business and capitalism.

As the odd state out in the election, Massachusetts became an easy target for conservative ridicule and a symbol of liberal righteousness. Republicans and others took to referring to the commonwealth as the "People's Republic of Massachusetts." Democrats and their allies, on the other hand, took a kind of sanctimonious pride in the state's rejection of Nixon, particularly as the Watergate scandal began to unfold. Bumper stickers declared, "Nixon 49, America 1," or more famously, "Don't Blame Me, I'm from Massachusetts."

Less than two years after his landslide victory, Richard Nixon faced impeachment in Congress and almost certain removal from the White House. On August 9, 1974, he became the first U.S. president to resign his office. The citizens of Massachusetts found it difficult to resist shouting, "We told you so!"

97

1976

A photograph of an antibusing demonstration photograph wins Pulitzer Prize.

IN 1965, A STATE COMMITTEE DETERMINED THAT A racial imbalance existed throughout Boston's public school system. Rather than address the problem, however, the Boston School Committee, chaired by Louise Day Hicks, ignored the commonwealth's findings. As a result, "racial imbalance" increased.

Finally, fed up with institutional discrimination and relying on *Brown v. Board of Education* for precedent, a group of black parents in Boston joined the NAACP in suing for redress in Federal District Court in March 1972.

A year later, a lengthy opinion by Judge W. Arthur Garrity declared that Boston's schools were "unconstitutionally segregated."

Garrity's ruling set in motion a process that would inevitably implement busing as a way to integrate the schools. That is, students would be bused from one section of the city to another, in an effort to integrate schools; racial quotas determined placement. No court was powerful enough, though, to mandate citizens' cooperation in such a plan.

In the working-class Irish Catholic neighborhoods of South Boston and Charlestown, residents resisted what they called "forced busing." They portrayed themselves as victims of social engineering perpetrated by "outsiders" and by a legal system unfairly tilted against them.

In their wrath, many white residents kept their children home from school as busing began in September 1974. Some organized protest marches and demonstrations; others threw stones at school buses carrying black students to previously all-white schools. Their anger was focused not only against blacks, the obvious racial target, but also against "one of their own"— Sen. Edward Kennedy, who had nominated Garrity for the federal bench and who had declared his support for court-ordered busing.

On September 9, 1974, Kennedy arrived at a City Hall rally of busing opponents to explain his position. He first was heckled, then chased off the stage. Kennedy escaped the crowd by hurrying inside the nearby Government Center federal office building named for his brother John.

Seven months later, on April 5,1976, anti-busing demonstrators once again came to vent their anger at City Hall Plaza. Into their midst marched Ted Landsmark, an attorney and executive director of the Contractors' Association of Boston, a trade group representing African Americans in the city's building industry. The demonstrators—mostly white high school students—could not resist the temptation to make a scapegoat of Landsmark. They surrounded him, knocked him to the ground, and kicked him.

As Landsmark rose to defend himself, a man carrying an American flag on a pole raced toward him. Among those watching was Stanley Foreman, a *Boston Herald* photographer. He framed the sickening scene in his lens just as the white figure with the flagpole speared his defenseless black vic-tim. Landsmark suffered a broken nose and other injuries. The shocking image deeply shamed a city that once touted itself as the Cradle of Liberty. Foreman's photograph won a Pulitzer Prize and focused national attention on the racial unrest in the city.

98

1990

Thieves remove paintings worth $200 million from the Isabella Stewart Gardner Museum.

LIKE WOLVES DRESSED IN SHEEP'S WOOL, THE ART thieves wore police badges and uniforms. On Sunday, March 18, 1990, at 1:15 A.M., a pair of bogus policemen banged at a side door to the Isabella Stewart Gardner Museum in Boston. They yelled to the guards inside that there was a report of a suspicious disturbance in the area, and they asked to be let in.

Within minutes, the feckless museum guards were prisoners bound with electrical tape, and the museum's sophisticated surveillance system was disabled. In the language of 1940s comic books, the "phony flatfoots" went to work. They spent two hours inside the Gardner before vanishing like smoke from a chimney. Eleven paintings by European masters—each universally agreed to be priceless—were carried off into the Fenway night, along with an ancient Chinese bronze.

Gone was *The Concert* by Jan Vermeer, the seventeenth-century Dutch artist whose entire known body of work numbers only thirty-two paintings. Ripped from its frame was *A Lady and Gentleman in Black* by Rembrandt as well as a self-portrait etching and *The Storm on the Sea of Galilee*, Rembrandt's only seascape. Gone, too, were *Landscape with an Obelisk* by Rembrandt's pupil Govaert Flinck; *Chez Tortoni* by Edouard Manet; and five pieces by Edgar Degas. A Shang

Dynasty (1200–1100 BCE) bronze beaker, the museum's most ancient object, was also taken.

Pressed to place a dollar figure on the theft, museum officials determined the pieces were worth more than $200 million (today the FBI places their value near $300 million), a figure that made the Gardner theft the most lucrative art heist in history. The museum had not insured the works, as the premiums would have been higher than the $2.8 million operating budget could handle. The theft was the most sensational in the art world since the 1911 lifting of the *Mona Lisa* from the Louvre. (The Leonardo da Vinci masterpiece was recovered two years later.)

Art specialists wondered whether the thieves had a specific "shopping list." Why leave behind a Rubens or a Giotto or a Raphael or some other more important Rembrandt? Some suggested that the stolen art was intended for an eccentric Japanese collector. Others theorized that the paintings would be used by Colombian drug dealers as a commodity form of payment, an alternative to cash. FBI agents hunted for clues inside the museum, while curators waited to receive a ransom demand.

The thieves, however, have proven reticent. To date there is still no trace of them or the abducted art. The $1 million reward offered by auction houses Christie's and Sotheby's remains unclaimed.

The well-known terms of Mrs. Gardner's will—that every object in her house remain as it was when she died, or else the museum's entire contents must be sold—remain faithfully observed. Paintings, sculpture, and objets d'art are not shielded behind Plexiglas nor otherwise protected. Despite the theft, the art that the notable Bostonian collected in her lifetime is as vulnerable as ever.

2001

Hijackers seize a pair of airliners bound from Boston to Los Angeles.

FEW DAYS EVER HAVE BEGUN SO BEAUTIFULLY AND ended so horribly as Tuesday, September 11, 2001. Across New England that morning, the late-summer sky was cloudless and the air as clear as glass. At 8:00 A.M., American Airlines Flight 11 climbed from a runway at Boston's Logan International Airport into the crystal blue sky; fourteen minutes later, United Airlines Flight 175 likewise rose toward the heavens. Both planes were making transcontinental voyages to Los Angeles, and on board were a total of 137 passengers and 20 crew.

The departures seemed typical for a weekday morning—but not for long. According to air traffic control transcripts, Flight 11 ceased regular communications with the ground at 8:14, following a routine course adjustment. The Boeing 767 was headed west, just over the Massachusetts–New York border, when the crew no longer answered air traffic controllers and the plane's transponder (an automatic radio device relaying altitude and position) stopped transmitting. At 8:24, any doubt that Flight 11 had been hijacked vanished when controllers heard a voice declare to the plane's passengers, "We have some planes. Just stay quiet and you will be OK. We are returning to the airport." But the plane was not returning to the airport. It was on a course to intersect Tower 1 of the World Trade Center at the lower end of Manhattan. The voice probably belonged to Egyptian-born Mohammed Atta, one of five terrorists on board the plane.

For Flight 175, the play of events was eerily similar. Also a Boeing 767, it was following a westward course across Massachusetts. And like Flight 11, it had five hijackers among its passengers. The pilot even made visual contact with Flight 11, and at air traffic control's orders, steered clear of the other commandeered jet. At 8:41, Flight 175 fell into radio silence, and five minutes later, someone had turned off its transponder, too. Saudi-born Marwan al-Shehhi was now in control.

At 8:46, a second pair of jet aircraft took off from a Massachusetts airfield: U.S. Air Force F-15s out of Falmouth's Otis Air National Guard Base. The scrambled fighter planes were battle-ready and heavily armed. Over New York City's skyline, however, events came to a climax quickly: At 8:48, Flight 11 slammed directly into Tower 1 (also known as the North Tower, and home to the "Windows on the World" restaurant on the 107th floor). Janitors, cooks, office clerks, and executives struggled to comprehend what had occurred and how—or whether—they might escape, while firefighters fought to defeat the jet-fuel flames. Yet the incredible happened again. At 9:03, Flight 175 hurtled like a missile into Tower 2.

New York City absorbed the hardest blows of the September 11th terrorist attacks. Both landmark World Trade Center towers collapsed to the earth that morning into a heap of rubble, and more than 2,600 people lost their lives (not including those on the airliners). Hundreds more also died as another hijacked airliner struck the Pentagon in Washington, and still another—thought also to be headed to the nation's capital—crashed into the ground outside Shanksville, Pennsylvania. Of every other state in the Union, though, Massachusetts seems closest to the abominable events that day. For in our skies, ordinary aircraft were transformed into terrible instruments of death.

100 | 2005?

The modern world's largest and most costly urban public works project, "the Big Dig," ends.

WHEN BOSTONIANS SPEAK OF THE "BIG DIG," THEY refer to a $15 billion highway and tunnel construction project in the heart of downtown Boston. For three very small words, the Big Dig—officially, the Central Artery/ Tunnel project (CAT)—encompasses various ambitious undertakings whose size and scope stagger the non-engineer's mind.

To date, the Big Dig has already extended the nation's longest highway, Interstate 90, to its long-intended final destination at Logan International Airport, via the Ted Williams Tunnel running under Boston Harbor. (I-90 now runs coast to coast, linking Boston and Seattle.) The Big Dig has also seen construction of the world's widest cable-stayed bridge. Named for a local civil rights activist as well as the nearby Revolutionary War battle site, the Leonard P. Zakim Bunker Hill Bridge has given Boston a new signature landmark. Most dramatically, the Big Dig has also replaced the elevated six-lane Central Artery with a network of subterranean eight- and ten-lane roads.

To make way for the Big Dig, the Central Artery has vanished, though it has gone without the slightest lament. The notorious roadway was conceived in the early 1950s, just ahead of the birth of the federal interstate highway system. State-funded, the $110 million construction project proved an eyesore even before it opened in 1959. Thousands of offices, stores, and homes fell to the wrecking ball to make way for steel and concrete. Large areas of downtown were split apart, as if an earthquake had cleaved the ground. Even from behind the wheel of an automobile, the four-mile stretch of the Central Artery was a nightmare: traffic congestion clogged its narrow lanes and myriad exits, making for frequent collisions.

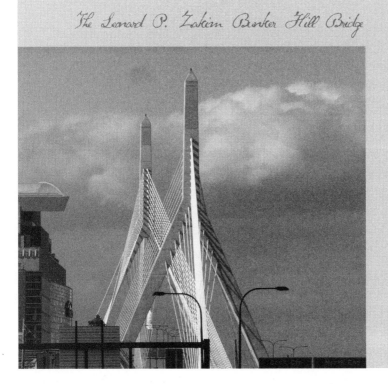

The Leonard P. Zakim Bunker Hill Bridge

By the late 1970s and early 1980s, politicians and bureaucrats united for a second bite at the transportation apple in Boston. Frederick P. Salvucci, who was State Secretary of Transportation for Gov. Michael Dukakis, is credited as the first to envision the Big Dig as a single, massive project uniting two long-dreamed-of schemes: the depression of the Central Artery, and creation of the "third" harbor tunnel to Logan Airport. A native Bostonian and MIT-trained civil engineer, Salvucci planned to achieve all this without razing any homes or closing any businesses.

Dukakis, who originally opposed the tunnel but had long supported the depression of the Central Artery, eventually gave his backing to Salvucci's vision in 1983. Perhaps most important, the CAT project—it had not yet earned its nickname—then found a powerful friend in U.S. Congressman Thomas P. O'Neill, Jr., a Democrat whose district covered a large portion of the proposed construction site.

As Speaker of the House, "Tip" O'Neill wielded great influence on a heavily Democratic Capitol Hill, but he encountered fierce opposition to the Big Dig from Republicans and leading members of the Reagan administration.

O'Neill introduced legislation authorizing federal funding for the project in 1984 and left office two years later without seeing it pass. In 1987, however, Sen. Edward Kennedy succeeded in overriding a Reagan veto by threatening a North Carolina colleague with the loss of tobacco subsidies.

The detours have been many, and the road network downtown has seemed to change monthly, yet the promise of a Big Dig without any Big Expulsion has largely come to pass. Indeed, the project has gone far to improve Boston's neighborhoods. Millennium Park, on the banks of the Charles River in West Roxbury, and the Boston Harbor Islands, to name only major examples, benefited from Big Dig landfill and state-of-the-art environmental recovery work.

The end of the Big Dig is really only the end of a chapter and not the conclusion of an entire story. With the Central Artery a memory, Bostonians must decide how to erase the scar left behind. Many believe the best way to do so is with a so-called green belt of parks like Olmsted's Emerald Necklace; others would rather see a redevelopment effort that would rebuild old neighborhoods and create new ones. Upon reflection, in fact, "Big Dig" seems a fine nickname for Boston as a whole, just as New Orleans is "the Big Easy," and New York City is "the Big Apple." Without an endless series of "big digs" going back long before the filling of Back Bay, and certain to continue well past the conclusion of "the Big Dig," the city of Boston would truly not exist.

101

2005

Massachusetts is home to World Series and Super Bowl winners.

IN CONTEMPORARY PROFESSIONAL SPORTS, FEW teams enjoy consistent good fortune. The New York Yankees, of course, dominated major league baseball for a good part of the last century. In football, the winning ways of the Dallas Cowboys once earned them acclaim as "America's Team." Yet most lineups, no matter which game they play and no matter how beloved by their fans, typically achieve nothing more than mediocrity.

Only the Boston Red Sox ever gained notoriety—and even a kind of affection—for their ongoing failure to win the World Series. The departure of Babe Ruth to New York after the 1919 season marked the beginning of the drought. With his pitching and his hitting prowess, Ruth had made the Red Sox a powerhouse on the baseball diamond for most of the decade. In fact, he helped take the Sox to three Series wins, in 1915, 1916, and 1918. For more than eighty years after his exit, however, the World Series title always eluded the Sox, no matter how well they played or how loudly the Fenway faithful cheered.

By the 2004 season, though, the team and New England baseball fans were thoroughly prepared to relinquish misfortune as a birthright. "This is the year," they vowed. And with the likes of Curt Schilling, Manny Ramirez, Pedro Martinez, Jason Varitek, and Derek Lowe, the Sox made good on that promise on October 27, 2004, after a four-game sweep of the St. Louis Cardinals. Even more exciting was their remarkable string of four victories against their archrivals the Yankees to take the American League Championship after falling behind three games to none.

On October 30, a crowd estimated by some to total 3 million lined a three-mile parade route through downtown Boston to welcome home the winning nine. The "Curse of the Bambino" was reversed at last. Among those millions, surely, were those who asked themselves, "How can it get any better?"

It could, and it did. On February 6, 2005, in their third NFL championship in four years, the New England Patriots defeated the Philadelphia Eagles 24–21 in Super Bowl XXXIX. Led by coach Bill Belichick, the Pats—with quarterback Tom Brady and kicker Adam Vinatieri, who once again secured the winning three-point margin—started the season as champs and ended it with another parade through the streets of Boston.

As this book went to press, before the 2005 baseball season, Boston—famous for so many reasons—was also the undisputed champion in America's leading professional sports.

Bring on the next parade!

Bibliography

Aesculapian Boston: A Guide to Places of Medical Historical Interest. Boston: Paul Dudley White Society, 1980.

Amory, Cleveland. *The Proper Bostonians*. New York: E. P. Dutton, 1947.

Avrich, Paul. *Sacco and Vanzetti: The Anarchist Background*. Princeton, N.J.: Princeton University Press, 1990.

Axelrod, Alan, and Charles Phillips. *What Every American Should Know About American History*. Holbrook, Mass: Adams, 1992.

Bailey, F. Lee, with Harvey Aronson. *The Defense Never Rests*. New York: Stein & Day, 1971.

Bearse, Ray, ed. *Massachusetts: A Guide to the Pilgrim State*. Boston: Houghton Mifflin, 1970.

Beatty, Jack. *The Rascal King*. Reading, Mass.: Addison-Wesley, 1992.

Behn, Noel. *Big Stick-up at Brink's*. New York: G. P. Putnam's Sons, 1977.

Benson, Richard, and Lincoln Kerstein. *Lay This Laurel*. New York: Dover Books, 1973.

Benzaquin, Paul. *Fire in Boston's Cocoanut Grove*. Boston: Branden Press, 1959.

Bishop, Jim. *The Days of Martin Luther King, Jr.* New York: G. P. Putnam's Sons, 1971.

Blanchard, Paula. *Margaret Fuller: From Transcendentalism to Revolution*. New York: Delacorte Press, 1978.

Boettinger, H. M. *The Telephone Book*. Croton-on-Hudson, NY: Riverwood Publishers, Ltd., 1976.

Bradford, William. *Of Plymouth Plantation*. New York: Modern Library College Editions, 1981.

Brant, Irving. *The Bill of Rights: Its Origin and Meaning*. Indianapolis, Ind.: Bobbs-Merrill, 1965.

Brown, Richard D. *Massachusetts: A Bicentennial History*. New York: W. W. Norton, 1978.

Butterfield, Roger. *The American Past*. New York: Simon & Schuster, 1947.

Chase, Owen. *Narratives of the Wreck of the Whale-Ship Essex*. New York: Dover, 1989.

Clark, Judith Freeman. *From Colony to Commonwealth*. Northridge, Calif.: Windsor Publications, 1987.

The Commemorative Guide to the Massachusetts Bicentennial. Dublin, N.H.: Yankee, 1975.

Conuel, Thomas. *Quabbin: The Accidental Wilderness.* Amherst: University of Massachusetts Press, 1981.

Covey, Cyclone. *The Gentle Radical: Roger Williams.* New York: Macmillan, 1966.

Creamer, Robert W. *Babe: The Legend Comes to Life.* New York: Penguin Sports Library, 1974.

Cumming, William P. *Seafaring in Colonial Massachusetts.* Boston: The Colonial Society of Massachusetts, 1980.

Curtis, Edith Roelker. *A Season in Utopia: The Story of Brook Farm.* New York: Thomas Nelson & Sons, 1961.

Derderian, Tom. *The Boston Marathon.* Champaign, Ill.: Human Kinetics, 1994.

Dickey, Glenn. *The History of the World Series Since 1903.* New York: Stein and Day, 1984.

Douglas, Frederick. *Narrative of the Life of Frederick Douglass, an American Slave.* New York: Penguin Books, 1987.

Edmonds, Anne Carey. *A Memory Book: Mount Holyoke College, 1837-1987.* South Hadley, Mass.: Mount Holyoke College, 1988.

Faber, Doris and Harold. *We, the People: The Story of the United States Constitution.* New York: Charles Scribner's Sons, 1987.

Farr, Francine, and Lee Rand. *A Diary of the Visits of Frederick Douglass to Nantucket Island.* Boston: The Museum of Afro-American History and the Nantucket Atheneum, 1991.

Federal Writers' Project. *WPA Guide to Massachusetts.* New York: Pantheon Books, 1983 (originally published in 1937).

Frank, Gerold. *The Boston Strangler.* New York: New American Library, 1967.

Franklin, John Hope, and Alfred A. Moss, Jr. *From Slavery to Freedom.* New York: McGraw-Hill, 1994.

Frederickson, George M., ed. *Great Lives Observed: Wm. Lloyd Garrison.* Englewood Cliff, N.J.: Prentice-Hall, 1968.

Gillmer, Thomas. *Old Ironsides.* Rockport, Me.: International Marine, 1993.

Greene, John. *Creation of the Quabbin Reservoir: The Death of the Swift River Valley.* Athol, Mass.: Transcript Press, 1981.

Haley, Alex. *The Autobiography of Malcolm X as told to Alex Haley.* New York: Random House, 1964.

Harris, Leon A. *Only to God: The Extraordinary Life of Godfrey Lowell Cabot*. New York: Atheneum, 1967.

Higgins, David. *Portrait of Emily Dickinson: The Poet and Her Prose*. New Brunswick, N.J.: Rutgers University Press, 1967.

Holmes, Pauline. *A Tercentenary History of the Boston Public Latin School*. Cambridge, Mass.: Harvard University Press, 1935.

Hopkins, Donald R. *Princes and Peasants, Smallpox in History*. Chicago: University of Chicago Press, 1983.

Howe, Henry. *There She Is, Behold Her*. New York: Harper & Row, 1971.

Jackson, Robert B. *The Gasoline Buggy of the Duryea Brothers*. New York: Henry Z. Walck, 1968.

James, Henry. *The Bostonians*. New York: Bantam Books, 1984 (originally published by Macmillan, 1886).

Johnson, Frederick. *The Boylston Street Fishweir*. Andover, Mass.: Papers of the Robert S. Peabody Foundation for Archaeology, 1942.

Johnson, Thomas. *Emily Dickinson: An Interpretive Biography*. New York: Atheneum, 1955.

Keller, Helen. *The Story of My Life*. New York: Airmont, 1965.

Kennedy, Lawrence. *Planning the City upon a Hill: Boston Since 1630*. Amherst: University of Massachusetts Press, 1992.

Kent, David. *The Lizzie Borden Sourcebook*. Boston: Branden Publishing, 1992.

The Martin Luther King, Jr., Companion. New York: St. Martin's Press, 1993.

Kirker, Harold, and James Kirker. *Bulfinch's Boston*. New York: Oxford University Press, 1964.

Labaree, Benjamin Woods. *The Boston Tea Party*. New York: Oxford University Press, 1964 (repr., Boston: Northeastern University Press, 1979).

Langguth, A. J. *Patriots: The Men Who Started the American Revolution*. New York: Simon & Schuster, 1988.

Lehman, Milton. *This High Man: The Life of Robert H. Goddard*. New York: Farrar, Straus, & Giroux, 1963.

Lieb, Frederick G. *The Boston Red Sox*. New York: G. P. Putnam's Sons, 1947.

Linden-Ward, Blanche. *Silent City on a Hill*. Columbus: Ohio State University Press, 1989.

Lowell, the Story of an Industrial City: A Guide to the Lowell National Historic Park. Washington, D.C.: National Park Service.

Lukas, J. Anthony. *Common Ground.* New York: Random House, 1985.

Manchester, William. *One Brief Shining Moment.* Boston: Little, Brown, 1983.

Marson, Philip. *Breeder of Democracy.* Cambridge, Mass.: Schenkman, 1963.

Mason, Julian, ed. *The Poems of Phillis Wheatley.* Chapel Hill: University of North Carolina Press, 1989.

Messerli, Jonathan. *Horace Mann.* New York: Alfred A. Knopf, 1972.

Middlekauf, Robert. *The Glorious Cause.* New York: Oxford University Press, 1982.

Miller, Perry. *Jonathan Edwards.* New York: W. Sloane Associates, 1949.

___, ed. *The American Puritans: Their Prose and Poetry.* Garden City, N.Y.: Anchor Books, 1956.

Morison, Samuel Eliot. *History of Harvard University.* Cambridge, Mass.: Harvard University Press, 1935.

Morgan, Edmund S. *The Birth of the Republic, 1763-1789.* Chicago: University of Chicago Press, 1956, 1977.

Oates, Stephen B. *Let the Trumpet Sound: The Life of Martin Luther King, Jr.* New York: Harper & Row, 1982.

O'Connor, Thomas H. *Bibles, Brahmins, and Bosses.* Boston: Trustees of the Boston Public Library, 1991.

___. *Building a New Boston.* Boston: Northeastern University Press, 1993.

Reid, William J., and Herbert G. Regan. *Massachusetts: History and Government of the State.* New York: Oxford Book, 1956.

Richmond, Merle. *Phillis Wheatley.* New York: Chelsea House, 1988.

Roman, Joseph. *King Philip: Wampanoag Rebel.* New York: Chelsea House, 1992.

Roper, Laura Wood. *F.L.O.: A Biography.* Baltimore: Johns Hopkins University Press, 1973.

Russell, Howard S. *Indian New England Before the Mayflower.* Hanover, N.H.: University Press of New England, 1980.

Schapp, Dick, ed. *Babe: The Legend Comes to Life.* New York: Penguin Sports Library, 1974.

Smith, Edward Conrad, and Harold J. Spaeth, eds. *The Constitution of the United States, with Case Studies,* 12th ed. New York: Barnes & Noble Books, 1987.

Smith, Philip Chadwick Foster. *The Empress of China*. Philadelphia: Philadelphia Maritime Museum, 1984.

Smith, Robert. *Babe Ruth's America*. New York: Thomas Y. Crowell, 1974.

Snow, Edward Rowe. *Romance of Boston Bay*. Boston: Boston Printing, 1944.

Starkey, Marion. *The Devil in Massachusetts*. New York: Alfred A. Knopf, 1949.

Swift, Lindsay. *Brook Farm: Its Members, Scholars, and Visitors*. New York: Macmillan, 1900.

Szatmary, David P. *Shays' Rebellion: The Making of an Agrarian Insurrection*. Amherst: University of Massachusetts Press, 1980.

Tharp, Louise Hall. *Mrs. Jack: A Biography of Isabella Stewart Gardner*. Boston: Little, Brown, 1965.

Tourtellot, Arthur Bernon. *The Charles*. New York: Farrar & Rinehart 1941.

Utley, Robert Marshall and Wilcomb E. Washburn. *Indian Wars*. New York: American Heritage Library, 1977.

Ward, Geoffrey C., with Ken Burns and Ric Burns. *The Civil War*. New York: Alfred A. Knopf, 1990.

Uleston, George. *Boston Ways*. Boston: Beacon Press, 1957.

Whitehill, Walter Muir. *Boston: A Topographical History*. Cambridge, Mass.: Belknap Press, 1959, 1968.

Wildes, Karl L., and Nilo A. Lindgren. *A Century of Electrical Engineering and Computer Science at MIT, 1882-1982*. Cambridge, Mass.: MIT Press, 1985.

Williams, Selma R. *Divine Rebel: The Life of Anne Marbury Hutchinson*. New York: Holt, Rinehart, & Winston, 1981.

Winslow, Ola Elizabeth. *John Eliot: "Apostle to the Indians."* Boston: Houghton Mifflin, 1968.

Winsor, Justin. *The Memorial History of Boston, Including Suffolk County, Massachusetts, 1630-1880*. Boston: J. R. Osgood, 1880-81.

Yool, George Malcolm. *1692 Witch Hunt: The Layman's Guide to the Salem Witchcraft Trials*. Bowie, Md.: Heritage Books, 1992.

Zobel, Hiller B. *The Boston Massacre*. New York: W. W. Norton, 1970.

Zophy, Angela Howard, ed. *Handbook of American Women's History*. New York: Garland, 1990.

Index

Abbott, Senda Berenson, 127
abolitionism and abolitionists, 76; Adams, John Quincy, 63; Missouri Compromise, 72–73; *The Commonwealth* (newspaper), 80; Garrison, William Lloyd, 81–82; *The Liberator* (newspaper), 81, 100, 102; Anti-Slavery convention, 93–95
Adams, Abigail, 61–62
Adams, Henry, 63
Adams, John, 37, 42; at first Massachusetts Constitutional Convention, 54–55; home of, **62**; political career, 61–64
Adams, John Quincy, 63
Adams, Samuel, 40, 59; and Sons of Liberty, 38, 42, 45; at Lexington and Concord, 46–48; at first Massachusetts Constitutional Convention, 55
African American poet, first published, 107–109
African American regiment, nation's first, 107–109
Aiken, Howard, 157–158
Alcott, Bronson, 89, 92, 111–112
Alcott, Louisa May, 111–112
Algonquian language, 27
Algonquians, 3, 9
Allen, Ethan, 53
American Federation of Labor (AFL), 142–143
American Revolution. *See* Revolutionary War
American Tragedy, An (Dreiser), 121
Amherst, MA, 123–124
Amistad (Spanish slave ship), 63
Andrew, John, 108
anesthesia, first use in surgery, 97–99
Antinomians, 25
Aquidneck Island, 16
Arbella (Puritan flagship), 12
Attucks, Crispus (Michael Johnson), 41–42
Auburn, MA: launch of first liquid-fuel rocket, 148–149

Back Bay, Boston, 103–105, 104, 123
Bailey, F. Lee, 171–172
baseball: Boston Pilgrims, 134–136; Boston Red Sox, 146–147, 154–155, 183–184
Basketball Hall of Fame, **126**, 127
basketball, invention of, 125–127
Battle of Bunker Hill, 49–51
Beacon Hill, 11, 59–61
Bell, Alexander Graham, 118–119
Big Dig, the, 181–183
birth control, development of, 166–167
Blackstone (Blaxton), Rev. William, 10–11
Blackstone River, 11
Blithedale Romance, The (Hawthorne), 92
blue laws, 23
Borden, Lizzie, 127–129
Boston: name origin, 13; smallpox epidemic of 1721, 32–34; burial reform, 83–85; Back Bay, 103–105, 104, 123; fire of 1872, 113; Emerald Necklace park system, 121–123; Boston Athletic Association (BAA), 131–133; first subway system in America, 133–134; molasses flood, 141–142; police strike of 1919, 142–143; Cocoanut Grove

nightclub fire, 155–156; reelection of Mayor James Michael Curley, 158–160; Brink's Robbery, 160–162, 161; first successful human kidney transplant, 162–164; racial imbalance in public schools, 175–177; Big Dig, 181–183
Boston Common, 11; public punishment on, 24; subway system, 133–134
Boston football, 115–116
Boston Latin School, 16–17
Boston Manufacturing Company, 68–69
Boston Marathon, 131–133
Boston Massacre, 41–42, **42**
Boston Pilgrims, 134–136
Boston Public Garden: Ether Monument, **99**; development of, 105;
Boston Red Sox: sale of Babe Ruth, 146–147; Ted Williams, 154–155; 2004 World Series win, 183–184
Boston Strangler, the, 170–172
Boston Tea Party, 40, 44–45
Boston's Committee of Safety, 46
Boylston, Dr. Zabdiel, 34
Bradford, William, 7–8
Bradley, Milton, 106
Brahmins, 75–77, 132
Braintree, MA, 62
Brandeis, Louis Dembitz, 138–140
Brandeis University, **139**, 140
"Bread and Roses" strike, 136–138
Breed's Hill, Charlestown, 50, 77
Brigham and Women's Hospital (Peter Bent Brigham Hospital), 162–164
Brink's Robbery, 160–162, **161**
Brook Farm Institute of Agriculture and Education, 91–93
Brooke, Attorney Gen. Edward, 171
Broughton, Nicholson, 52
Bryant, Gridley, 78
Bulfinch, Charles, 17, 59–61
Bunker Hill, Battle of, 49–51
Bunker Hill Monument, 77–79
burial reform, 83–85
Burns, Anthony, 101–103
busing, court-ordered, 175–177

Cabot, John, 4
Calvinism, 75–76
Cambridge, MA: Harvard College, 18–19; first e-mail sent, 172–173;
Cape Ann, 6
Cape Cod, 4: name origin, 5; Pilgrims and, 7; cranberry industry, 70–72
Cape Cod Bay, 5
Carney, William, 109
Carver, John, 8
Catholicism, and politics, 168–170
censorship, 120–121
Central Artery/Tunnel Project, 181–183
Champlain, Samuel de, 5
Channing, William Ellery, 76

Charles River, 6, 47, 69
Charles River Museum of History, 69
Charlestown, 11, 12, 13, 19, 47; Battle of Bunker
    Hill, 49–51; Bunker Hill Monument, 77–79
Charlestown Committee of Safety, 47
Chase, Owen, 74–75
Chase, William Henry, 75
"Checkered Game of Life, The," 106
China trade, 56–57
Christian Science, 116–118
Christmas, sanctioning by Puritans, 23
Church, Benjamin, 29
Clark University, 148–149
Cockenoe, 27
Cocoanut Grove nightclub fire, 155–156
Coffin, Dr. John Gorham, 83–85
Commonwealth Avenue, **104**
"Commonwealth" of Massachusetts, defined, 55
Compromise of 1850, 102
computers, Mark I, 157–158
Concord, MA: American Revolution, 46–49; North
    Bridge, **48,** 48–49; Walden Pond, 95–97; Alcott
    family, 111–112
Congregationalism, 76
Connecticut River Valley, 2, 87
Constitution of the Commonwealth of Massa-
    chusetts, 54–56
Constitution, USS (frigate), 65–67, **66**
contraception, development of, 166–167
Coolidge, Calvin, 142–143
Copley, John Singleton, 39–40
Cotton, John, 14
cranberry farming, 70–72, **71**
Curley, James Michael, 158–160, **159**

Dana, MA, 152–153
Danvers Witch Memorial, **31**
Darrow, Clarence, 121
Dartmouth (tea ship), 45, 46
Davy, Sir Humphrey, 98
Dawes, William, 46–47
De Salvo, Albert, 171–172
Dedham, MA, 27
desegregation of schools, 175–177
Dial, The, 89–90
Dickinson, Emily, 123–125; home of, **124**
Dorchester Heights, 49–50, 53
Douglass, Frederick, 93–95, 100, 102, 107
Du Bois, W. E. B., 109–111
Duryea, Frank and Charles, 129–131
Duryea Motor Wagon Company, 131
Dyer, Mary, 25

e-mail, first, 172–173
East Chelmsford (Lowell), MA, 69
East India Company, 44–45
Eddy, Mary Baker, 116–118; home of, **117**
education: Boston Latin School, 16–17; Harvard
    College, 18–19; establishment of public educa-
    tion system, 20; Perkins School for the Blind,
    79–80; establishment of state board of education,
    85–86; Mount Holyoke College, 87–88, 89
education reform, 85–86
Edwards, Rev. Jonathan, 34–36
Eliot, Charles, 140

Eliot, Rev. John, 26
Emerald Necklace park system, 121–123
Emerson, Ralph Waldo, 17, 76, 89, 91, 96
Empress of China (cargo ship), 56–57
Enfield, MA, 152–153
Essex (whaler), 74–75
ether, first use in surgery, 97–99
Ether Monument, **99**

Fall River, MA: Lizzie Borden murders, 127–129
Faraday, Michael, 98–99
Farrakhan, Louis, 164–166
Federalists, 61
feminism. *See* women's rights
Fens, the, 123
fires: great fire of 1872, 113–114; Cocoanut Grove
    nightclub fire, 155–156;
Fisher, Dr. John, 79–80
Fitzgerald, John "Honey Fitz," 169
football: "the Boston game," 115–116; New England
    Patriots, 183–184
Foreman, Stanley, 176–177
Forrester, Jay, 157, **158**
Foster, Stephen and Abby Kelly, 101
Franklin, Benjamin, 38, 54
French and Indian War, 37–38
Fruitlands, 112
Fugitive Slave Act, 102
Fuller, Margaret, 89–90, 92

Gage, Thomas, 50
Gallows Hill, 31
Gardner, Isabella Stewart, 105
Gardner Museum, 177–179, **178**
Garrison, William Lloyd, 81–82, **82,** 95, 100
Garrity, W. Arthur, 176
Garvey, Marcus, 165
Georges, Capt. Robert, 10
Gerry, Elbridge, 64–65
"gerrymander," the, 64–65
Glover, Gen. John, 51–52
Goddard, Robert H., 148–149
Good, Sarah, 31
Gosnold, Bartholomew, 4–5
Granite Railway Company, 78–79
"Great Awakening," 34–36
Great Barrington, MA, 109–110
Great Boston Fire of 1872, 113–114
Great Hurricane of 1938, 151–152
"Great Migration," 12–13
Green, Capt. John, 56–57
Green Mountain Boys, 53
Greene, Nathanael, 51
Greenwich, MA, 152–153
Guerriere (British frigate), 66

Hale, Sarah Josepha, 10
Hall, Capt. Henry, 70–72
Hancock, John, 40, 43; and Boston Tea Party, 45; at
    Lexington and Concord, 46–48
Hannah (war ship), 51–52
Harvard College, **19**; founding of, 18–19; football
    at, 115–116, 143;
Harvard, John, 18–19
Hawthorne, Nathaniel, 92–93

Herrick, Ronald and Richard, 162–164
Holmes, Oliver Wendell, 67
Howe, Julia Ward, 80
Howe, Dr. Samuel Gridley, 79–80
Howe, Gen. William, 50, 53
hurricane of 1938, 151–152
Hutchinson, Anne Marbury, 14–16, **15,** 17, 25
Hutchinson, Thomas, 37, 45
Hutchinson, William, 14

Ice Age, 1–2
Industrial Revolution, 67–69
Industrial Workers of the World (IWW), 137–138
industry: iron production, 21–22, 22; textiles, 67–69,
   68, 136–138, 137; cranberry farming, 70–72, 71
inoculation, smallpox, 32–34
Intercollegiate Football Association, 116
internal combustion engine, 129–131
International Planned Parenthood Foundation, 167
ironworkers, 21–22
Isabella Stewart Gardner Museum, 177–179, **178**
Islam, Nation of, 164–166

Jamaica Pond, 123
Jefferson, Thomas, 54, 61, 73
Johnson, Ban, 134–136
Jones, Margaret, 30

Keller, Helen, 80
Kennedy, John Fitzgerald, 168–170; birthplace of, **169**
Kennedy, Sen. Edward, 176
Kidney transplant, first successful, 162–164
Killilea, Henry, 136
King Philip (Metacom), 28
King Philip's War, 28–29
Knox, Henry, 17, 53

labor reform: "Bread and Roses" strike, 136–138; and
   Louis Dembitz Brandeis, 140
Lawrence, MA: "Bread and Roses" strike, 136–138
Leonard P. Zakim Bunker Hill Bridge, 181, **182**
Lexington, MA: and American Revolution, 46–49
liquid-fuel rocket, first launched, 148–149
Little Women (Alcott), 112
Logan International Airport, Boston, 179
Lowell, A. Lawrence, 149–150
Lowell, Francis Cabot, 68–69
Lowell, MA, 69
Lowell Committee, and Sacco-Vanzetti case,
   149–150
Lyon, Mary, 87–89

Malcolm X, 164–166
Mann, Horace, 85–86
Marblehead, MA, 51–52
"Mark I" computer, 157–158
Martha's Vineyard, 5
Massachusetts Bay Company, 12
Massachusetts Constitution, 54–56
Massachusetts General Court: and founding of
   Harvard College, 18; and public education sys-
   tem, 20; and construction of State House, 60
Massachusetts General Hospital, 99
Massachusetts State House, 59–61, **60**
Massasoit, Chief, 9, 28

Mather, Rev. Cotton, 17, 33–34
Maverick, Samuel, 10
Mayflower, 6–8, **7**
Mayflower Compact, 8
McCormick, Katharine Dexter, 166–167
McDermott, John, 131–133
McGovern, George, 174–175
medicine: inoculation, smallpox, 32–34; anesthesia,
   first use in surgery, 97–99; first kidney transplant,
   111; development of contraception, 166–167
Melville, Herman, 74–75, 86
Middlesex Canal, 69
Mill Dam, 104–105
Milton Bradley Company, 106
Minutemen, 46, 47–49
Missouri Compromise, 72–73
Moby Dick (Melville), 74–75
molasses flood of 1919, 141–142
Monroe Doctrine, 63
Morton, William Thomas Green, 99
Mott, Lucretia, 100
Mount Auburn Cemetery, 83–85, **84**
Mount Holyoke College, 87–89, **88**
Muhammed, Elijah, 164–165
Muhammed's Mosque II, 164–166, **165**
Murray, Dr. Joseph, 163

Naismith, James, 125–127
Nantucket Island, 93–95
Narragansett tribe, 28–29
Natick, MA, 27, 29
National Association for the Advancement of
   Colored People (NAACP), 110, 175
Nation of Islam, 164–166
Native American tribes, 3, 9, 28–29; and Pilgrims,
   7–10
Needham, MA, 27
New England Patriots, 183–184
New England Society for the Suppression of Vice,
   120–121
New England Watch and Ward Society, 120–121
Newton, MA: Stanley Motor Carriage Company,
   131
Nipmuc tribe, 28–29
Nixon, Richard, 168, 170, 174–175
North Bridge, Concord, MA, **48,** 48–49
Northampton, MA, 35
Nurse, Rebecca, 31

"Old Ironsides" (USS *Constitution*), **66,** 66–67
Old South Meeting House, **114**
Olmsted, Frederick Law, 121–123
Onesimus, 33
Osburne, Sarah, 31
Otis, James, 36–37

Paleo-Indian hunters, 2–3
Parker, Theodore, 92, 102
Parris, Alexander, 77
Parris, Elizabeth, 30–31
Parris, Rev. Samuel, 30–31
Passos, John Dos, 150
Pawtuxet tribe, 9
Perkins, Thomas Handasyd, 78, 80
Perkins School for the Blind, 79–80

Philip, King (Metacom), 28
Phillips, Wendell, 17, 100
Pilgrims, 6–10
Pincus, Dr. Gregory, 166–167
Pitcairn, Maj. John, 48
Pleistocene Ice Age, 1–2
Plimoth Plantation, 9
Plymouth, MA, 6, 8–9
Pocasset tribe, 29
Pocumtuc tribe, 28
Poems on Various Subjects, Religious and Moral
    (Wheatley), 44
police strike of 1919, 142–143
politics, and religion, 168–170
Pollard, Capt. George, 74–75
Ponzi, Charles, 144–145
Ponzi schemes, 144–145
Pormort, Philemon, 17
power looms, 67–69
Prescott, MA, 152–153
Prescott, Dr. Samuel, 46–47
Prescott, Col. William, 50
Preston, Capt. Thomas, 41–42
Provincetown Harbor, 5, 7
public punishment/hangings, 24–25
Puritanism, 14–15; and education, 17, 18; laws, 23;
    decline of, 75–76; New England Society for the
    Suppression of Vice, 120–121
Puritans: arrival at Massachusetts, 11, 12–13; views
    on education, 20; and ironworkers, 21–22; sanc-
    tioning of Christmas, 23; and Quakers, 25; reli-
    gious conversion of Native Americans, 26–27;
    and Salem witch trials, 30–32

Quabbin Reservoir, 152–153, **153**
Quakers, 24, 25
Quincy, MA, 63

Red Sox: sale of Babe Ruth, 146–147; Ted Williams,
    154–155; 2004 World Series win, 183–184
Redcoats, 47–51, 52–54
Rehoboth, MA, 29
religion, and politics, 168–170
religions: Puritanism, 14–15, 17, 18, 23, 75–76,
    120–121; Calvinism, 75–76; Unitarianism,
    75–77, 92; Congregationalism, 76; Universalism,
    76; Christian Science, 116–118; Catholicism,
    168–170
Revere, Paul, 40, 41, 59, 65; midnight ride, 46–47
Revolutionary War: Lexington and Concord, 47–49;
    Battle of Bunker Hill, 49–51; George
    Washington and the *Hannah*, 51–52; British
    evacuate Boston, 52–53
Ripley, George and Sophia, 91–93
Robert Gould Shaw/54th Regiment Memorial, **108**
Roxbury Latin School, 27
Ruth, George Herman ("Babe"), 146–147

Sacco, Nicola, 149–150
Sachs, Henry, 148–149
"Sacred Cod," 4
Salem Village, 30
Salem witch trials, 30–32
Salvucci, Frederick P., 182
Samoset, 9

Sanger, Margaret, 166–167
Saugus Iron Works, 21–22, **22**
school desegregation, 175–177
Science and Health (Eddy), 117
September 11 terrorist attacks, 179–180
Shaw, Col. Robert Gould, 107–109, **108**
Shawmut Peninsula, 10–11, 103
Shays, Daniel, 57–58
Shays's Rebellion, 57–58
Sherborne, MA, 27
slavery, 56, 72–73, 81; Fugitive Slave Act, 102. *See
    also* abolitionism and abolitionists; slaves
slaves: Onesimus, 33; Phillis Wheatley, 43–44;
    Frederick Douglass, 93–95, 100, 102, 107. *See
    also* abolitionism and abolitionists; slavery
smallpox, 32–34
Smith, Capt. John, 5–6, 9
Society of Friends, 24, 25
Sons of Liberty, 38, 42, 45
Souls of Black Folk, The (Du Bois), 109
South Hadley, MA, 87–88
Spectacle Island, 33
Springfield, MA, 58; Milton Bradley Company, 106;
    Naismith Memorial Basketball Hall of Fame,
    126, 127; and gasoline-powered automobile,
    129–131
Squanto, 9
Stamp Act, 37–38
Standish, Capt. Miles, 7
Stanley Steamer, 131
state board of education, establishment of, 85–86
Stratton, Samuel W., 149–150
subway system, 133–134
Sugar Act, 37–38
Super Bowl, New England Patriots win, 183–184
Supreme Court, 138–140
surgery, anesthesia first used in, 97–99
Suttle, Col. Charles, 101–102
Swampscott, MA: Mary Baker Eddy home, 116, 117
Swansea, MA, 29
Swift River Valley, 152–153

Taft, William Howard, 139
Tallmadge, James, 73
Taunton, MA, 29
"Taxation without representation is tyranny," 36–37
taxes: Stamp Act and Sugar Act, 37–38; Tea Act,
    44–45
technology: power looms, 67–69; internal combus-
    tion engine, 129–131; liquid fuel rocket, 148–
    149; Mark I computer, 157–158; first e-mail sent,
    172–173
Temple School, 111–112
Tewksbury (Wamesit), MA, 29
textile industry, 67–69, 68, 136–138, 137
Thanksgiving, first, 9–10
Thayer, Judge Webster, 149–150
Thompson, David, 10
Thoreau, Henry David, 11, 86, 95–97; house at
    Walden Pond, **96**
Ticonderoga, cannons of, 53
Tisdale, Elkanah, 64
Tituba, 31
Tomaszweski, Stanley, 156
Tomlinson, Ray, 172–173

Townshend Acts, 38
trade, China, 56–57
Transcendentalism, 76, 89–90, 111

Union Army, 54th Regiment, 107–109
Unitarianism, 75–77, 92
Universal Negro Improvement Association,
    164–165
Universalism, 76
utopian communities, 91–93, 112

Vanzetti, Bartolomeo, 149–150

Wadsworth, Rev. Charles, 124
Walcott, Louis (Farrakhan), 164–166
Walden Pond, 11, 95–97
Walden (Thoreau), 97
Waltham, MA: textile mills, 67–69, 68
Waltham Watch Company, 69
Wampanoag tribe, 9, 29
War of 1812, 67
Ward, Gen. Artemus, 50
Ward, John Quincy Adams, 99
Warren, Dr. John C., 99
Warren, Dr. Joseph, 49–50
wars: King Philip's War, 28–29; French and Indian
    War, 37–38; American Revolution, 47–54; War
    of 1812, 67; Civil War, 107–109
Washington, George, 10, 36, 44, 51–54
Watson, Thomas, 118–119

Wellesley, MA, 27
Wells, Dr. Horace, 99
West Roxbury, MA, 93
Weymouth (Wessagusset), MA, 10
Wheatley, Phillis, 43
"Whirlwind," digital computer, 157–158
Willard, Solomon, 77–78
Williams, Abigail, 30–31
Williams, Ted, 154–155
Wilson, Woodrow, 138–140
Winthrop, John, 12–13, 17, 21
witchcraft, 30–32
Woman's Rights Convention, first national,
    100–101
women's rights: Margaret Fuller, 89–90; first nation-
    al Woman's Rights Convention, 100–101; devel-
    opment of contraception, 166–167
Wonders of the Invisible World, The (Mather), 33
Worcester Foundation for Experimental Biology,
    166–167
Worcester, MA, 100–101
World Series: first, 134–136; 2004 Red Sox win,
    183–184

X, Malcolm, 164–166

Young, Cy, 135

Zakim Bridge, 181, 182